CRITICAL
OPTIONS
FOR
EVANGELICALS

Also by Brian C. Stiller

Generation Under Siege

CRITICAL

OPTIONS

FOR

EVANGELICALS

from the Editor-in-Chief of Faith Today

Brian C. Stiller

Foreword by John H. Redekop

Faith Today Publications is the publishing division of the Evangelical Fellowship of Canada.

Acknowledgment is made to the following for permission to reproduce copyrighted material:

Lyrics from "Dressing Up Jesus" by Ralph Carmichael, © 1970 BudJohn (ASCAP) Songs. Used by permission of C.M.I., Nashville, Tennessee.

Scripture quotations taken from THE HOLY BIBLE, NEW INTERNATIONAL VERSION, © 1973, 1978, 1984 by International Bible Society. Used by permission of Zondervan Publishing House. All rights reserved.

Printed and bound in Canada by John Deyell Company

Canadian Cataloguing in Publication Data
Stiller, Brian C.
      Critical options for evangelicals

ISBN 0-9695596-0-7

1. Evangelicalism – Canada.   2. Church and the world.   I. Title.

BR1642.C3S75 1991   261'.1   C91-095336-8

Faith Today Publications
#1, 175 Riviera Drive
Markham, Ontario, Canada
L3R 5J6

To my friend
Bernice Boyes
for her courage and vision

Contents

PART TWO – CHRISTIANS AND THE PUBLIC ARENA

Foreword

SOME BOOKS SERVE as a mirror, others as a penetrating light. This slim volume does both. In these succinct analyses of wide-ranging issues, Brian Stiller has described dominant evangelical assumptions and interpreted key evangelical concerns. He has, in fact, gone a long way in defining contemporary evangelicalism while at the same time demonstrating reasons for its vibrancy.

While these thirty-three thoughtful essays individually constitute significant reflections, taken together they help the reader to understand the re-emergence of Canadian evangelicalism as a major force in society. Brian explains, analyses, describes and grapples with basic concerns. Time and again, with boldness and clarity, he challenges secular and humanist views. But he also prods evangelicals to translate beliefs into action, especially other-oriented action.

In the latter sense, this book constitutes a call to Christians to be relevant and to become involved. As he sharpens the issues, the author communicates a burden. He points out that all too often, in the moral struggles of the day, the evangelical church has been an observer rather than a participant. It has been rightly concerned with personal piety but unjustifiably mute in the face of profound social evil. Some readers may become uncomfortable as they delve into Brian's provocative challenges but, as they reflect on the realities, they will surely become more motivated than upset.

The author tackles numerous tough questions. Should evangelicals support Christian political parties? Should Christian teaching and prayers in public schools be a high priority? Does evangelicalism correlate closely with any political ideology? When should Christians practise civil disobedience? Is feminism anti-Christian? How should evangelicals advance values in a secular society?

At times the author's perceptive phrasing precipitates a reflective pause. "While materialism does not necessarily deny the reality of eternity, it always suppresses its importance." That's "quote-worthy." In similar vein we read, "If a church cannot talk about life after death, is there any reason to trust what it says about life before death?"

On occasion an earthly emphasis strikes home. "I wonder how many Canadian churches budget as much money for evangelizing youth in their community as they do for cleaning supplies." But one also encounters theological (and logical) gems. "Better to explode myths today than live with lies for a lifetime."

There is no shortage of specific admonitions, both direct and implied. "To avoid politics . . . is not being courageous but weak." And again, "My concern is that Christians don't simply mouth the opinions of the world without respect for the Word." All too often, warns Brian, "we operate as just another agency, meeting the agenda of the world that wants the benefit of Christ's love without

Christ's analysis or remedy." Not letting caution dilute integrity, the author states: "It shouldn't surprise us that Jesus so quickly forgave the sins of prostitutes and yet was devastating in his condemnation of the so-called religious leaders. For often it's the religious who hide under a lie of propriety, pretending to be who they aren't."

Perhaps Brian is at his best in his informed and provocative critique of the Rushton-Suzuki confrontation. Apparently it takes an alert non-scientist to tell the high-profile scientists to practise responsible science. Equally impressive, however, is the excellent analysis of the abortion question, especially of Bill C-43 with its moral shortcomings.

In sum, this timely publication by the executive director of the Evangelical Fellowship of Canada constitutes the best window on Canadian evangelicalism presently available. Providing a clear picture of the Canadian evangelical scene, it deserves a wide readership, not only among evangelicals, both leaders and laity, but also among critics, journalists, and the general public. Naturally no church or public library should be without it.

JOHN H. REDEKOP
Professor of Political Science
Wilfrid Laurier University
Waterloo, Ontario

Preface

MY LIFE HAS been lived in the shadow of the church. I was raised in a minister's home, studied for the ministry and then chose to serve the church in youth ministry and as a staff member of a national inter-church association.

What I love about the church is its ability to nurture, heal and shape lives. Those lives, in turn, are to move out into the world, filled with God's Spirit to set loose Christ's kingdom.

These essays have been written out of that world view. They first appeared in *Faith Today*, a Canadian evangelical news/feature magazine, and *Sundial*, a newsletter for members of the Evangelical Fellowship of Canada.

The readers I have written for in these two publications tend to be those with an evangelical Protestant commitment. However, I am increasingly driven to speak to a wider audience. I too become trapped into speaking only to those of my church and Christian ethos.

That being said, my focus in this book is twofold. Throughout, I examine, from a Christian perspective, the concerns of our post-modern society. But I also look at the effects of these concerns on our faith communities.

My prayer is that God would push us out to deal with the surrounding needs. That will lead us to engage the culture in Christ's name and power.

I am indebted to those who assisted me editorially. They include Lori Gwyn, Audrey Dorsch, Richard Mitchener, Anne James, Marianne Meed and Beth Jost.

The evangelical community is faced with a challenge to introduce biblical faith back into our culture. What will we do?

That challenge identifies the critical options facing our Canadian evangelical community.

BRIAN C. STILLER
Newmarket, Ontario
September, 1991

CRITICAL
OPTIONS
FOR
EVANGELICALS

Part One
OUR EVANGELICAL IDENTITY

1
Just Who Do We Think We Are?

The making of Canadian heroes

I LOVED TO WATCH Pete Rose play baseball. Crouching at the plate with bat in hand he was the embodiment of athletics – intense, committed and competitive. Then he was charged with violating baseball rules by betting on baseball games.

I sat on the edge of my chair as Ben Johnson ran at the 1988 Olympics in Seoul. I wasn't sure if my interest in his winning was my Canadian nationalism or because I wanted someone to whip Carl Lewis. When the report of Ben's using steroids surfaced I wanted to believe that the report was false.

If our growing disillusionment about sport heroes isn't enough, we are served with other examples of fallen heroes: business tycoons using insider trading to amass millions; one evangelist, while condemning another, trapped by his own sexual failings; politicians peddling their influence for money; priests sexually violating boys.

3

Our belief in leaders is shattered. While we want to believe, we are understandably gun-shy; whom can we trust? Mixed up with our feelings about leaders is our need for heroes. The two are intertwined.

I hoped Rose wasn't guilty. I wanted to believe the unfolding story of an evangelist's failings was nothing but a vicious media smear. And I was sure Johnson had been drugged by a villain.

These were public figures we looked up to. We expected something of them. And when they failed, our respect turned to bitterness and anger. Is it because we see something of ourselves in them? That when they fail, we fail?

A community, culture and civilization need heroes; that is, those who exemplify who we are, who point us in the right direction and inspire us to greater achievement.

We need our own heroes: people from our own soil who epitomize our beliefs and ideals and whose plans call for our support.

Hebrews 11 outlines those who stood for the rising spiritual identity of the Hebrew people. Although the foibles of Israel's heroes are not described in this brief mention in Hebrews, the Old Testament tells all. Biblical heroes were not free from moral failings. In fact, the basis of their influence was not perfection, but duty, risk and endurance.

Abraham lied to the king of Egypt about his beautiful wife Sarah to save his own neck. Isaac was a deceitful scoundrel. Moses was violent; Rahab was a prostitute; Gideon at first was a coward; Samson was controlled by lust and David broke more laws than most.

Were they acceptable because of their sins? No, they were accepted in spite of them. Essential to the impact of their stories is the reality that God chooses imperfect people who are willing.

A fickle view of the south

Canadians, living on the border of a world power with which there are historic, cultural and ethnic links, have traditionally looked south for many of their ideas and heroes.

How convenient. If the shine of an American hero is tarnished, there is a predictable cultural defence: "Well, after all, that's an American for you."

It's here that the strange reality of Canadian caution takes over. We reject what appears to be idolatrous American hero worship. And rightly so. Revelations of misdeeds by popular religious leaders lend legitimacy to that rejection. But at the same time, the rejection of the American model of hero worship generates a reluctance to stand behind Canadians.

Canada has relatively a small population and thus a smaller pool of heroes; its citizens often show jealousy when someone else succeeds; and its leaders are reluctant to support one another.

Both the House of Commons and Legislative Assemblies operate on the basis of political caucuses. That is, the members are required to vote according to party lines. This intensifies partisan politics.

Unfortunately that same mentality affects the church, where denominationalism is such a powerful caucus that possible initiatives are sometimes torpedoed simply because the idea or the leadership came from another group. Further, over the past few decades the social movement of egalitarianism (the search for equality) has made inroads in the church, leading many to believe that the only way to lead is by committee. This idea has been supported by the increased dominance of government, big business, as well as unions, and a growing body of laws regulating everything from human rights to corporate dealings tends to diminish risk-taking in leadership.

Servant leadership

Mixed into the debate is an anaemic view of servant leadership. While lipservice is often given to the concept, in reality servanthood gets reduced to the status of a doormat. But true servant leadership works when people follow a leader who truly serves. This model of servanthood also precludes the religious John Waynes who swagger off alone with no accountability.

The balance lies between the two extremes – mindlessly worshipping a personality and ignoring those called to lead. The story is told of an elderly woman who, on hearing that Lester B. Pearson had won the Nobel Peace Prize, asked, "Just who does he think he is?" Failure to affirm our leaders stems from the Canadian penchant to downgrade our nation. Nationalism, like individualism, can lead to idolatry. But not to take our country seriously is to say God has no plan for nationhood.

Canadian novelist Scott Symon wrote, "Canadians are, after all, simply romantics who lost the courage of their hopes." I pray he is wrong.

To engender courage among youth, courage must be expected. To expect risk-taking, risk-taking must be fostered. To raise up capable and trustworthy leaders, ability and responsibility must be affirmed. Cynicism is not a fruit of the Spirit. Like other forms of worldliness, it only inhibits the workings of God in our land.

**Failure to affirm our leaders
stems from the Canadian penchant
to downgrade our nation.**

2
Passing the Torch

Are we preparing capable Joshuas to follow in Moses' steps?

STAR TREK, THE POPULAR TV series, proclaims its continuing mission, " . . . To seek out new life . . . to boldly go where no one has gone before!"

Can such a statement be said of our faith? Or has life become so technical, our faith so doctrinal, ministry so systematized, leadership so disappointing and our dreams so tarnished with fatigue and cynicism that our hearts no longer thrill to the challenge of taking new territory for God?

This I asked as I stood to speak at a conference for younger church leaders from around the world.

My analysis was that church leadership following World War II was characterized by creativity and risk-taking. In turn, my generation was recruited into managing the visions of those of the former generation. The long shadows of those whose visions we managed shielded us from developing our inner dreams. Instead, we seemed to enjoy the security and comfort of continuing with their ideas and organizations.

A world survey

A few years ago I travelled to many parts of the world and discovered the same patterns I had observed in North America. I saw little effort anywhere by senior leaders to pass the torch to younger leaders (and to my surprise, little interest by younger leaders to pick up the torch). Although senior leadership recognized the desperate need for younger leadership, there seemed to be little effort to put in place a strategy for raising up a new generation of leaders.

But even more frightening was the drift of younger leaders in many countries and for various reasons. Many were simply looking for positions that would provide social standing and financial security.

I also saw people reworking old leadership models – holdovers from the colonial experience. Inflexible denominations and stereotyped organizational patterns were squelching creativity.

A critical question for every denomination and organization is, "To whom will you pass the torch of leadership?"

When we fail to pass the torch

It's obvious that many churches and Christian organizations today need torch passing. Failure to pass on leadership is often due to leaders holding on too long with little attempt to train or give opportunity to the younger. Or, the tension between the two age groups produces so much conflict that younger leaders head off to other, more flexible opportunities.

This is especially evident in church denominations as younger people walk away and join faster moving parachurch agencies. As a result, energy and vision are suppressed.

How can the torch be passed? Does it take a revolution for leadership to wake up? Or, are tension and the suppression of talent and ideas necessary to force a change?

There is a wonderful example in the Old Testament of torch passing: Moses to Joshua. The announcement, "Moses, my servant, is dead," boomed out across the valley. What would happen? many wondered. Not to worry: Moses had prepared one who could carry the torch – Joshua.

Moses' ideas are germane for this generation. The Old Testament patriarch recognized that leadership emerges out of different styles. Whereas he was a crusader, Joshua was a manager. Moses, angered by the treatment of his kinsfolk, killed an Egyptian. Later he defended young women who were being harassed while tending their sheep. Ultimately his crusader instinct led him to say yes to God's call to lead God's people out of Egypt.

How different was Joshua. Right from the beginning he was obedient. Never was there any conflict with Moses. There was no sign of a strident spirit or self-centred personality.

Neither did Moses look for someone like himself. A different style was needed. Moses' and Joshua's backgrounds, personalities, styles, means of operation and public profiles were vastly different. Yet each was every bit a leader.

Also, each out of his strengths and gifts, was used by God in a particular way and particular time.

Different times call for different styles

It's easy to be trapped into believing there's a "best" form of leadership. My generation grew up thinking its garments had to be cut from a certain cloth, that leaders should be aggressive, charismatic and individualistic. But this model of leadership, suited to its time and culture, surely is not the only one there is.

Moses, a restless and dominating figure who led his people out of bondage, gave definition to the structures and laws of the community because of his special contact with God. How different was Joshua! Learning from his tutor he accepted the patterns and ideas of his predecessor and moulded them into a working society. Each leader was competent; their styles were different.

Passing the torch is inevitable

Making the transition from one generation to the next is tough. My generation has lived with the "long shadow" syndrome. That's when a key senior leader – often a creative and crusading "Moses" – continues for so long that his or her shadow blankets the one following. As a result, the up and coming leader doesn't get an opportunity to nurture his or her own vision. Instead, the younger leader gets trapped by serving the older, never developing the fine edges of his or her own leadership.

Managing Moses' ideas

Joshua wasn't Moses and he didn't try to be. Indeed, he became the manager of Moses' ideas. But the reason Joshua succeeded was that he refused to succumb to the weakness which plagues all managers: maintaining the status quo. Instead he nurtured his own vision and was willing to take risks beyond the old borders defined by Moses.

Canadians were captured by three unlikely heroes during the 1980s. Terry Fox, with one leg lost to cancer, ran half way across Canada. Steve Fonyo, who had also lost a leg to cancer, completed the cross-Canada run. And Rick Hansen rolled 40,000 kilometres around the world in his wheelchair.

Canadians responded with uncharacteristic enthusiasm. Why? Because the unlikely opposed their natural handicaps and defied those who were able.

Our society is possessed with itself. Sadly, the church is infected by the same spirit. It's time for some heroes. It's time to run counter to the plague of "me first." It's time to run with the torch.

Our world is in need of women and men of God who will lead His people into His promises. This does not call for passive, timid-minded souls. It will take those who, like Joshua, in faith and Christ-like grace follow on the heels of mighty leaders and pick up the torch.

**Younger leaders can get trapped
by only serving the older,
never developing the fine edges
of their own leadership.**

3

Wanted: Radicals for Our Time

A call to authentic, biblically-based living that upsets the status quo

EVER SINCE HE walked the earth, Jesus has inspired radicals: from the Apostle Paul and Francis of Assisi to John Knox and Martin Luther and others.

Today I'm looking for genuine contemporary radicals. And I don't mean religious lunatics who, in absurd or obnoxious style, attract attention. I remember too well, as a teenager in Saskatoon, being embarrassed by a "Christian" group who arrived in town and quickly landed in the local jail. They said it was because they were evangelizing. In fact they drove up and down 2nd Avenue, screaming out Bible verses. They got what they deserved while we slipped away, hoping no one would associate us with them.

What I'm looking for is more than noticeable behaviour. And for sure, it's not a new gospel.

Out of our emerging generation we need women and men who will upset the status quo of conventional, complacent, secular thought and be authentic, biblically-based radicals.

William Wilberforce

One of the most powerful lessons of history comes from William Wilberforce. A politician in England, first elected in 1780, he gave his life to the abolition of slavery.

In retrospect we say, "how noble." But that opinion was not shared by many of his evangelical associates.

Charles Colson, in his book *Kingdoms in Conflict*, describes what Wilberforce encountered when he arrived to take up his seat in the House of Commons.

High society of the times was "one vast casino where the rich counted their profits through a fog of claret. Fortunes were lost and won over gaming tables, and duels of honour were the order of the day. The city's elegant private clubs welcomed young Wilberforce, and he happily concentrated on pursuing both political advancement and social pleasure . . .

"Crammed together in shabby dwellings, they were cogs grinding out a living in the Empire's emerging industrial machines. Pale children worked eighteen hours a day in cotton mills or coal mines to bring home a few shillings a month to parents who often wasted it on cheap gin."

Into that kind of world, a young politician risked his fame and future opposing slaves being transported from Africa to the Americas. Following his spiritual conversion and the subsequent influence by the former slave-trader John Newton (author of Amazing Grace), Wilberforce became a determined radical.

His friends thought he was crazy. Even his close friend, Prime Minister William Pitt, didn't understand. After a meeting with Pitt, Wilberforce reflected in his diary:

"Pitt tried to reason me out of my convictions but soon found himself unable to combat their correctness, if Christianity was true. The fact is, he is so absorbed in politics, that he has never given himself time for due reflection on religion."

There were times when it seemed everyone opposed Wilberforce, but none of them kept him from his mission. James Boswell, Samuel Johnson's biographer, wrote a snide poem ridiculing Wilberforce and did so by only giving the first letter of his name:

"Go, W with narrow skull,
Go home and preach away at Hull.
No longer in the Senate cackle
In strains that suit the tabernacle;
I hate your little whittling sneer,
Your pert and self-sufficient leer.
Mischief to trade sits on your lip,
Insects will gnaw the noblest ship
Go, W, begone, for shame,
Thou dwarf with big resounding name."

A group of associates, affectionately referred to as "The Clapman Sect," supported him in the fight.

In one of his last letters, John Wesley wrote to Wilberforce ". . . Unless God has raised you up for this very thing, you will be worn out by the opposition of men and devils, but if God be for you who can be against you? Are all of them together stronger than God? Oh, be not weary of well-doing. Go on in the name of God, and in the power of His might, till even American slavery, the vilest that ever saw the sun, shall vanish away before it."

Wilberforce did continue his struggle. It wasn't until February 22, 1807 that the House of Commons moved against slave trading. For Wilberforce, it took another 18 years of dogged determination to finally emancipate existing slaves.

We look back with admiration at such historical examples. But are the times much different today? I think not. We are surrounded by the same self-centred hedonism, materialism and religious egoism as was Wilberforce. There are current evils as destructive and horrifying as were slave trade and child labour.

Risking

Many Christians today are active, defying evil in Christ's name. But too often evangelicals simply stand on the sidelines expecting Roman Catholics such as Mother Teresa, or social liberals to defend the defenceless.

I get letters from people who say, "Yes, but did you read what Brother So-and-So said?" We must understand that to bring about change, it will take more than a few powerful sermons or pamphlets. It takes carefully constructed and funded strategies. It calls for an understanding that God's people – the laity – need to be released from internal church operations to be God's ambassadors in the public square as well. It also calls for churches, together in communities, to share human and fiscal resources, to correct the wrong and turn back evil.

In short, we need some flesh and blood models, men and women who will march to a different drummer, who live out the redeeming presence of Christ in full view of their neighbours. I think of Irene Kahler who, as a medical specialist, cares for AIDS patients in Calgary. Or pharmacist Henry Koop and his wife Agnes who, volunteered their time to coordinate a crusade against tuberculosis in Haiti. Or Lilian Marshall, who loved the unlovely in Dorchester Penitentiary.

I hear much about AIDS being a punishment for the morally disobedient. But where are those who will bring healing and the love of Christ to those facing the final moments of life? We suffer under the collective guilt of 75,000 children aborted each year in Canada. Yet how much of our church budgets do we dedicate to helping those who assume their only two options are abortion or poverty? I hear many decry the high cost of taxes and government programs. But few do I see crafting plans to help the homeless find somewhere to live.

In short, I hear many voicing a biblical concern for our secular, self-centred world. Yet I find myself longing, not for the past, but for a new breed of Christians who will rise above the narcissism and ego-centred theology of our new-Evangelicalism and live out His righteousness.

I pray that Sir Samuel Romilly's tribute to Wilberforce would be the epitaph of the modern Christian: "When he should retire into the bosom of his happy and delighted family, when he should lay himself down on his bed, reflecting on the innumerable voices that would be raised in every quarter of the world to bless him; how much more pure and perfect felicity must he enjoy in the consciousness of having preserved so many millions of his fellow-creatures."

Change will take more than
a few powerful sermons or pamphlets.
God's people need to be released
to be present in the public square.

4
The Paradox of the Gospel: Free but Costly

What price do we pay for our faith?

SHE WAS QUIET and unassuming as we sat at lunch in Manila; she neither looked nor spoke like a hero. We were both participants at the 1989 Lausanne Congress on World Evangelization.

"How long were you in prison?" I asked, assuming it was at most a few weeks.

"Five years," she said quietly. Before anyone at our table could speak she continued, "Don't feel sorry for me. It was a wonderful opportunity of knowing Jesus through suffering and, as well, I was able to lead a number of prison guards to Christ."

I was stunned. Five years in prison in a Marxist African nation! It didn't take much effort to imagine what she would have experienced. And what was her crime? She had witnessed quietly of her faith.

What is the cost of the gospel? On missionary Sunday, cost is defined in terms of money: "How much can I give?" On dedication Sunday, when a son or daughter responds to the invitation to foreign service, cost is defined in terms of family: "What will I do if my child moves halfway around the world?" At an evangelistic service, when a person indicates a choice to follow Jesus, cost is defined in terms of relationships: "How will loved ones react to this choice?"

Our salvation cost Jesus Christ his life, and we are recipients of that free gift of salvation. It is free because nothing we had to offer was enough to pay our debt of sin. Thus Christ's death became the only account sufficient to make payment and cancel our obligations.

The flame of truth

But Christ's call does not end at that point. As inheritors of his life, we're called to live out the very nature of his life. We share in his adventure of bringing truth and life to a world inhabited by evil. In short, it's a call to keep alive the flame of truth.

Lighting the candle of truth may be truly heroic or painfully mundane. When Corrie Ten Boom and her family decided to resist the Nazi Secret Service and hide Jews in their home, it was heroic. For a teenager to refuse to laugh at a racist joke may seem uneventful. But in both cases there is a price paid. One may be life itself, but for a teenager to face the ridicule of a peer group, it may feel like death.

Dietrich Bonhoeffer, the German pastor who died in a volley of Nazi bullets, coined the phrase "cheap grace." It meant grace without cost, following Christ with only intellectual assent or holding correct doctrine but without living the Christ-like life.

"Cheap grace means the justification of sin without the justification of the sinner," he wrote in *The Cost of*

Discipleship. "Let the Christian live like the rest of the world, let him model himself on the world's standards in every sphere of life, and not presumptuously aspire to live a different life under grace from his old life under sin."

North American culture, and subsequently western evangelical subculture, has passed through a number of phases with respect to its view of life, luxury and license. A brief review of events of recent decades illustrates our growing dislike for costly faith.

Patterns of response

In the 1950s the evangelical world was caught in an anti-worldly form of legalism: "Don't smoke, drink or go to dances."

The revolutionary mood of the '60s, expressed in music, was countered by an anti-change conservatism among evangelicals: "Don't listen to modern music."

But during the '70s evangelicals underwent a radical shift. Instead of being *anti* we became *pro*. Instead of rejecting the cultural trends we accepted them. The "possibility thinking" of the '70s was reflected in a reworked agenda among evangelicals; many believed that whatever they wanted was what God wanted: "Since we are the King's kids, let's live like it."

During the 1980s disaffected minorities organized as they realized they had become socially and politically marginalized. So did evangelicals. Reacting to secularism, evangelicals tried to reassert their presence: "Since God is creator, His laws should be imposed on our nation."

The shift in the '70s and '80s reflects a desire to benefit from the application of the gospel rather than to give because of the gospel.

At stake is the Christ of our life who calls us to live out His life. There are times when that call may result in conflict with the prevailing culture. At other times it may lead us in its support. But at all times we are called to light the candle of His truth regardless of benefit or cost.

A Chinese pastor stood at the Manila conference and told of his 12 years of imprisonment. His job was to clean the cesspool of the prison camp. This daily chore of disposing of human faeces was not a curse as the prison guards had planned. Instead, for him it was a blessing. Because of the smell he was left alone, which allowed him to pray and sing out loud. His favourite refrain was, "I come to the garden alone, while the dew is still on the roses . . . And He walks with me and He talks with me and He tells me I am His own, and the joy we share as we tarry there, none other has ever known."

To serve five years in an evil prison or to clean cesspools for 12 years is a cost some pay today for their faithfulness. Our cost in the West may be different, but for those who are called, there is no exemption. The paradox of the gospel: It is free but costly.

At all times we're called
to light the candle of God's truth
regardless of benefit or cost.

5
Hell: The Great Denial

A theology of avoidance

THERE IS NOTHING like a funeral to force one to consider what happens after death. Gone from the body is any trace of life. The embalmers have guaranteed that.

"Where is he now?" I wondered, while attending the funeral service for a family friend. From my understanding of the Bible, I knew the answer: he was with the Lord.

But what if he had been an unbeliever?

While we hear frequent references to heaven from Christians and non-Christians alike, our culture avoids the subject of hell. Hell – as a place and as an idea – is loaded with too many negative images. And it triggers such anxious thoughts and fears that we avoid it in our conversations.

Hell is slipping from our theology. But we avoid this subject at our own peril. When was the last time you heard a sermon on heaven and hell? If you are a typical churchgoer, you'll likely answer, "Not very recently."

Sociologist Reginald Bibby, reviewing the Canadian religious scene, said, "Speaking sociologically and not theologically, I would suggest that the reluctance of Canada's religious groups to speak on the subject [of life after death] is a poignant commentary on the extent to which they have become spokespeople for culture rather than for the gods."

If a church cannot talk about life *after* death, is there any reason to trust what it says about life *before* death?

Before evangelicalism became an essentially middle-class religion, evangelicals were rightfully accused of resorting to "hellfire and brimstone" rhetoric.

Evangelist Billy Sunday, along with other colourful speakers, brought notoriety to the practice of frightening people with the unquenchable fire of everlasting punishment.

Today, if the occasional evangelist takes a run at the subject, he or she is sure to be quickly branded a raving fundamentalist by mainstream and more "moderate" Christians.

Our growing reluctance to engage in serious discussion about the eternal consequences of rejecting Jesus Christ stems from a number of factors, each of which may be expressed in the form of a commonly asked question.

#1. *Doubt: How could a loving God do it?*
The notion that a loving God would condemn a person to an eternal hell is repugnant. Hell, many think, is what we believed in when we were uneducated, trapped by a more literal interpretation of the Bible.

Today's increased theological emphasis on grace can tend to shift our attention away from the burden and consequences of human choice.

#2. Distraction: Doesn't God need good buildings?

Our present preoccupation with constructing and expanding new churches and ministry facilities indicates a shift in our priorities.

While we may protest that preparing for eternity is what we are all about, church budgets paint a different picture. The large amounts of our financial resources spent on buildings betray what's important to us. I don't dispute the need for quality architecture and adequate worship space. But our use of finances is a barometer indicating what we really believe.

#3. Timidity: How can you tell a friend?

It is difficult – many would say profoundly unkind – to tell people that their loved one who died without accepting Christ is in hell. If the deceased was a relative of the head deacon or elder, or even worse, a large financial donor, a pastor will be tempted to avoid mentioning eternal lostness at all.

#4. Materialism: So what's wrong with the good life?

Materialism is a belief that the high values in life are built around our material benefits and the comfort of life.

While materialism does not necessarily deny the reality of eternity, it always suppresses its importance. And so "believing in Christ makes me a more successful and a happier person" becomes the assumed wisdom, as well as the bait to lure the unconverted.

Evangelicals tend to absorb the surrounding worldly preoccupations. Parents expect their children to get a good education; to land a good job to ensure future success. If our young people drift away from middle-class values and show interest in something that may lead to an "insecure" future, we get nervous. Our view of life after death is obscured by our frantic search for the good life today.

#5. Universalism: Didn't he die for all?

Respectability is an unconscious desire of religious minorities. To be regarded as "fringe" or fanatical is something to be avoided. Hell seems to go with the territory, and hence, should be avoided.

One way around the dilemma is to believe in universalism: that everyone will eventually escape eternal lostness because Christ's sacrifice was sufficient for all. (C.S. Lewis, for all his orthodoxy in other areas, was sympathetic to this theory.)

Universalism is profoundly appealing: it softens the picture of a hard-hearted Father who condemns ordinary people to eternal damnation – just because they didn't accept Christ's payment for their sin. It also removes the fear of never seeing a loved one again. But it is unscriptural.

The evangelical drift

The danger facing the evangelical church is not so much in denying the Bible as in drifting away from critical emphasis in order to accommodate itself to the demands of the culture.

It's time we turned the attention of our community to life after death. Death is central to living. The gospel addresses the most basic aspects of living.

Materialism is wrong. Our universe is more than the physical one we can see. Our present life, once it has been lived, is finished. Neither is our life recycled into another through reincarnation. Time on this planet is no more. We move from here out into the fullness of God's order forever. And that is both the hope and caution of life. Life today counts. It has consequences. There is a heaven to gain and hell to shun.

This does not mean we are called to the rhetoric of fanaticism. To shock people unduly does not honour the integrity of God's Word or the workings of the Holy Spirit – it is God who does the saving. But to warn people "of the wrath to come" is surely our task. To do so helps focus priorities, both for our personal lives and the local church. And it offers to the nonbeliever an understanding of the ultimacy of life. We do people a service when we warn them of the peril of rejecting Christ and the hope of faith.

Eternity, wrote missiologist Don Richardson, is written on our hearts. Let us not fail this generation by avoiding the subject of hell.

**If a church cannot talk about
life after death,
is there any reason
to trust what it says about
life before death?**

6
A Christian Census

How many Canadians go to church?

SOMEONE STARTED A rumour that the United Nations had listed Canada as being non-Christian. In all of our attempts to verify this story, we found no UN documents to substantiate it. But the question remains: What is the state of the church in Canada?

We do know that the religious landscape is changing. A survey of secular bookstores tells that story. Religious sections are filled with New Age material. Statistics of church membership and attendance sound a shrill alarm, warning us that our country is not as it once was.

Before we throw up our hands in frustration, a picture of the Christian community would help us better understand what we face.

What do we mean by "Christian"?
What do we mean when we say someone is "Christian"? As an evangelical, my definition of a follower of Jesus

Christ is narrower than some would accept. For example, I don't believe that those born into a home in which the parents are committed Christians, are necessarily Christian.

Evangelical Protestant Christians are only a small percentage of those who identify themselves as followers of Christ. Thus to facilitate our understanding, I examine the church, beginning with the broadest definition down to an evangelical Protestant definition.

How many attend church?

First, let's look at the term "Christian" in the broadest sense, i.e., including all who say they are. In the 1981 census 11,402,605 claimed to be Catholic, 361,560 Eastern Orthodox and 9,914,580 Protestant. Out of a total of 24,083,495, a very high percentage claims to be Christian.

But it's not enough to ask what religious group people identify with. A vital question is how frequently they attend the church of their choice.

Asked that question, 27 percent of Protestants claimed to have attended their place of worship within the past seven days; 43 percent for Roman Catholics and Orthodox. Those percentages add up to 28 percent of Canadians claiming to have attended church in the previous seven days. (See *Fragmented Gods*, R. Bibby, Irwin, 1987.)

How many evangelicals?

Now to a much narrower definition: How many Canadian Protestants would consider themselves to be evangelical?

There are two points to be kept in mind. First, how many people attend Protestant churches that theologically and publicly align themselves as evangelical and, second, how many consider themselves evangelical but attend a

27

mainline Protestant church that would not identify itself as being evangelical.

This requires two assessments:

First, how many Canadians claim attachment to a church or denomination that is known as being evangelical? The total listed in the 1981 Census is 2,019,105.

Second, we should add to that number those in the mainline Protestant churches who would identify themselves as being evangelical. For this there are no studies. To arrive at that I've examined both Bibby's figures and those published by the Evangelical Fellowship of Canada's Vision 2000. (See *Reclaiming a Nation*, ed., A. Motz, 1990.) In my assessment, it would be on the low side to estimate that five percent of those attending a mainline Protestant church are of evangelical conviction. Five percent of 7,709,400 would come to almost 450,000.

Adding the 2,019,105 (those who say they belong to an evangelical Protestant church) to five percent of the mainline (450,000) totals approximately 2.5 million. I think it's safe to say that up to 10 percent of Canadians are affiliated in belief, worship and attendance to evangelical Protestantism.

But is Canada Christian?

But can Canada really be called Christian? We need to look at the other side of statistics. Less and less is Christian influence being felt in our land. During Christmas season, more and more politicians send words of holiday wishes with phrases like "season's greetings." Few include the word "Christmas." A teacher said she was not allowed to include anything related to Christ, including the word Christmas, in school festivities.

Christian ideas are under attack. They are being pushed

aside in the marketplace of this nation. We are faced with the need first to understand how Canadians lost their faith and then to develop a strategy to reach them with Christ.

Many evangelicals have laboured under two misconceptions. One is that if we convert enough people, then peace and righteousness will reign. But notice that in the United States, during the period in which the percentage of those who claimed to be "born again" was at an all-time high, the crime rate soared as did the increased incidence of abortion.

We also assume that the structures of society are neutral, unaffected by the presence of evil. The more complex our world becomes, however, the more we realize that political, educational, economic, legal and social decisions made by governing bodies have an incredible effect on us all. And if Christ's presence is absent from these structures, you can be assured that darkness will prevail.

Numbers are important. Indeed, let us work to touch more lives with Christ's transforming presence. Those who ignore the hard reality of numbers by saying they are irrelevant are fooling themselves. But numbers are only part of the picture. While we may increase the actual numbers of those who confess Christ, at issue is also the need to shape and influence our country through policies, laws and institutions which in turn influence all of our lives.

To ignore numbers is to be foolish. To deny the need to shape our country under God's laws is fatal.

Ten percent of Canadians are affiliated with evangelical Protestantism.

7
Do Evangelicals Evangelize?

It's time to re-examine our navigational maps

THE OLD SHIP of Zion needs a massive overhaul. The waters we thought we could fathom, and the rocks we believed we could avoid suddenly force us to re-examine our navigational maps. Scandals among leaders shake our credibility. Society has more ammunition than ever to discredit our mandate to evangelize. Our culture has been indifferent to Christ's claims, but now evangelicals face a widespread cynicism fuelled by scandals, squabbles and self-centred materialism.

But before we lay our troubles at another's door, there is a truth we must face. As evangelicals we've been coasting for a long time. We've assumed that since our theology is evangelical, we've been evangelizing. That simply isn't true. Statistics indicate that North Americans are losing their historical commitment to Jesus Christ.

There are external and internal reasons why our present situation calls for serious thought and bold strategy.

The changing sea

Our world is constantly and drastically changing. New currents of ideas, attitudes and responses are moving in. The shoals we thought we knew so well have shifted; new ones tear at the hull. Consider the following:

1. Television can distort – like a glass that magnifies small items into something larger-than-life. Some forms of worship, especially nonliturgical, emotional ones, are meaningful in the context of a church, but on the TV screen they can seem corny, insincere, or downright foolish.

TV also individualizes religion. Cameras focus in on one person. The more dramatic he or she is, the better the ratings. That can lead the viewer to identify biblical faith with the speaker, which amounts to idolatry.

2. Proselytizing (we call it evangelizing) is becoming culturally offensive. As our society becomes more pluralistic it assumes that since there are many faiths, no one faith can be more right than another. Indeed, political scientist Dr. Paul Marshall has predicted that in the not-too-distant future we may be challenged in court for evangelizing those of other faiths.

3. Our culture is losing interest in organized religion. A national study shows that only 14 percent of those between the ages of 15 and 24 indicate they value organized religion. Also, whereas 85 percent say they believe in a personal God, only 12 percent say they are influenced by God. So while many retain a warm-fuzzy feeling about God, when it comes to living, religion as a shaping force hardly rates.

Looking at the ship

The old ship Evangelicalism itself needs some reassessing.

* Credibility, one of the most powerful tools of the evan-

gelist, is at an all-time low. I cringe when the style of some TV evangelists borders on hucksterism.

* We are losing our "Billy Grahams." Powerful proclaimers have become scarce. That may be because we don't attach enough importance to the gift of preaching or enough funds to ensure it is nurtured.

How many of our Bible colleges and seminaries have chairs of evangelism? How much do local churches actually give to support evangelists?

* The evangelical church is becoming more self-focused. Our budgets and programs don't always indicate that winning the lost to Christ is our main goal. I wonder how many Canadian churches budget as much money for evangelizing youth in their community as they do for cleaning supplies?

* Evangelicals have climbed the rungs of the economic ladder, as our modern churches and state-of-the-art technology attest. There is nothing inherently wrong with being middle-class. The danger is that as we begin to think like those around us we begin to lose our distinctiveness. We focus on making people feel better, live better, raise better families, earn and save more money, get a better education – and the list goes on. Forgotten is the desperate state of people eternally lost without Jesus Christ.

The sea isn't our biggest challenge: it will always be rough. Our ultimate task is to ensure that our ship is seaworthy, equipped and managed so that we can reach those in need of salvation.

**As we think more like
people around us
we begin to lose
our distinctiveness.**

8
"Dressing Up Jesus"

Are we turning people off Jesus by how we represent Him?

RALPH CARMICHAEL, back in the heyday of the Jesus Movement, wrote,

> "Everyone 's dressing up Jesus.
> Style Him just like you want Him to be.
> Everyone's dressing up Jesus now.
> You're just seeing what you wanted to see.
> Let Him keep his sandals, robe and flowing hair.
> Now you add some red and yellow beads.
> Cover up the calluses, keep Him thin and fair.
> A little speech of love and peace is really all you need."

We are still "dressin' up Jesus" today, though maybe not in long hair or beads. Out of ethnic origins, cultural background, age or education, we interpret Jesus to match our expectations.

A recent book on religion in Canada (*God's Dominion* by Ron Graham) suggests that while people have an active

33

interest in religion, fewer are looking to organized religion. That's a sharp reminder that even though our church and parachurch budgets are expanding and our programs increasing, only a small percentage of this generation has any interest in what our church and religious organizations are trying to do.

In all of our attempts to portray a vibrant, caring, all-powerful Jesus, most people roll over Sunday morning, catch an extra hour of sleep and pass us off with a big yawn.

Is it Jesus they reject? Yes, often it is. Who He is and what He stands for cuts across self-centred interests, unbelief and arrogant worldliness. This we understand. As Scripture warns us, for many He is a rock of offence.

But it is not always "His fault." There are too many indicators that tell us people aren't always turned off by the person and message of Jesus but by how He is represented. At a Billy Graham crusade, a young person carried a placard, "Christ yes. Christianity no!"

The garb
Today many churches and missions are setting new goals of evangelism. As we step up our efforts to spread the good news, we would do well to examine the garb in which we wrap truth: to ask ourselves, Are we distorting Jesus by our packaging?

How we represent Jesus to others naturally flows from how we understand God ourselves. We're not the first to err by wrapping truth in our own garb.

Jonah did it. He was angry at God for withholding judgment on Ninevah. He believed that those violent, heathen Ninevites deserved punishment. After all, wasn't it Israel that had pioneered the notion of Jehovah? Wasn't

Israel the nation that should experience blessing and protection?

It wasn't that Jonah had too high a view of his nation. Rather, his view of God was too small. Jonah's God was wrapped in the flag of his nation. We call it fascism.

Solomon, the wise and prudent sage, descended into depression: "Meaningless! Meaningless! . . . Utterly meaningless! Everything is meaningless," he said. Like Jonah, his strength became his weakness. His brilliance and accomplishments brought him no joy. They had become ends in themselves rather than a means to the end of worshipping God. Solomon's God was wrapped in his own competence. We call it humanism.

What a shock it was for Peter, when in a dream God told him to eat what his religious tradition taught him was unclean. Then, to Peter's amazement, he was instructed to go to a Gentile's home and there share Jesus Christ. Steeped in narrow, religious dogmatism, he was convinced that because only a select few could expect to be receivers of God's grace, others should be ignored.

His doctrinal purity blinded him to the needs of others. Even more devastating, he failed to understand the breadth of God's heart. Peter's God was wrapped in religious sectarianism.

Some Bible scholars have suggested that Judas's willingness to sell Christ for 30 pieces of silver wasn't for the money, but was his attempt to force Jesus to use His power. Judas, like most Jews of his day, was looking for the Messiah to come and rid Israel of its enemies, to once and for all establish the throne of King David in full power and authority. If that was Judas's motivation then his God was wrapped in the flag of his own political ideology. We call it triumphalism.

The disciples were forced to deal with Simon the Sorcerer who tried to buy the gifts of the supernatural with money. The disciples saw through the self-interest of his ego and rejected his request. Today, people are attracted and seduced by claims to the supernatural. What draws a bigger crowd than a miracle? Jesus refused to perform a miracle for the Pharisees. Simon's God was wrapped in the spectacular garb of supernaturalism.

A mother, warning her daughter of possible pitfalls, said, "Stay away from drugs and evangelicals." Was she afraid her daughter would meet Jesus Christ? Or had her experience been so negative that the very idea of fervent faith filled her with anger? I don't know. But I can tell you that later the daughter, during a period of sorrow, met a pastor who introduced her to spiritual wholeness. Apparently the mother had been introduced to a convoluted Jesus. She reacted, whereas the daughter, encountering the loving, caring Jesus, opened up her life to him.

The essential Christ

While churches and denominations develop and launch their strategies, and writers and media consultants devise their material, we must remind ourselves of the essentials of people's needs. An old camp meeting song puts it clearly: "What the world needs is Jesus, just a glimpse of Him."

It was not wrong for Jonah to support his nation. God uses nations. Neither was it inappropriate for Solomon to utilize his ability. Peter had firm doctrinal ideas. Judas's alleged desire for his nation's liberation was legitimate. Simon's interest in true divine intervention was understandable.

Common to all these Bible characters is that they were

trapped into believing that the means of life and ministry were in fact the goals, that their particular context of faith formed the boundaries of who God was.

I was raised in a prairie parsonage in the 1950s. The music and cultural forms of that era and community have shaped my understanding of Christ and faith. My son and daughter are, in turn, learning life in their world. Their music, cultural forms and understanding of life are shaped by the technology and global transparency of their world. As much as I may want them to hear the gospel through the musical patterns of my own experience, that will not happen. If I try to force my experience on them, their reaction will not be so much to the person of Jesus but to my wrappings of Jesus.

Carmichael ended his song:
"Have you really seen Him?
Looked at Him straight on?
Can you take Him as He is,
With the trimmings and trappings gone?"

Most young people
roll over Sunday morning,
catch an extra hour of sleep
and pass us off with a yawn.

9
Sins of the Saints

While many criticisms seem unfair,
evangelicals do have points of vulnerability

DO EVANGELICALS DESERVE some of the negative press we've been getting recently? Here are a two examples.

"Love and Hate," a CBC drama on the life of Colin Thatcher, former Saskatchewan politician convicted of murder, was reviewed by CBC's The Journal. Thatcher was referred to as being "born again" and now an evangelical. The insinuation was that a person charged as a criminal had no business being forgiven and, by implication, those who did consider him forgiven (i.e., evangelicals) were obviously not very bright.

A television movie, "Money, Power, Murder", caricatured a white-suited television evangelist cavorting in a luxurious home with a beautiful woman (not his wife), manipulating people into a religious experience for his own purposes.

The question is, do we deserve it? Is the way these people view us an accurate and fair representation of who we are? Or is this some plot to discredit those who believe the Bible and trust in Jesus Christ as Saviour?

Danger signs

My reaction to this loading of negative connotation onto the label "evangelical" has been, "That's not fair." It would be easy to dismiss the criticisms as unreasonably biased.

But then a senior government official told me that when evangelicals are mentioned in government circles it is assumed that those being discussed are narrow-minded, bigoted, demanding and resistant to change.

While I know we are subject to false accusations, I have come to recognize points of vulnerability within our community. These are expressed in various ways and need identifying.

But first, there is, in my view, a reason that we evangelicals too often are seen to be against much in our world. We're called "conservative Protestants" because our theology is conservative. Those with a conservative world view, by definition, can become resistant to change: new ideas are rejected because they are seen to be new. Those with a conservative theology are inclined to conserve both their faith and practices of the past.

While that may be very good, a danger is that what may have been culturally relevant in the past may be completely irrelevant today. As well, each church has old policies which, even in their accepted day, were not in keeping with the spirit of Christ. But because they are part of one's heritage they are retained or conserved.

With that as a background, the following are some sins to which we evangelicals may be inclined. Not all evangelicals are guilty of these faults: but they are slopes down which we can too easily slide.

* *Racism*. Given our memory of Canada's Judeo-Christian heritage, there is a danger that as people move into Canada – especially from central Asia – importing their own religious systems, we may react. The argument is that since this country was founded on biblical ideas, newcomers should learn about our faith. But the danger is that our arguments may camouflage an underlying racist bias.

* *Sexism*. The feminist movement over the past 25 years has at times generated more heat than light. Strong feminist assertions, often based on a secular approach, too often seem to fly in the face of evangelical beliefs. Feminist support of abortion, homosexual rights and state intervention in family matters has angered many of us. This triggers a reaction that may trap evangelicals into not only opposing the secular views but also the legitimate biblical rights of women. This casts on us a pallor of being anti-women and male-chauvinistic.

* *Homophobia*. Unquestionably, most evangelicals oppose homosexual practice. But what we struggle with is separating the sin from the sinner. Just listen to the anti-homosexual jokes you sometimes hear Christians tell. Is it all in good fun or do you detect at its heart not only disagreement with but actual hatred of those who are homosexual?

* *The Poor*. Often those who are reasonably well off assume that in our modern society there are basically three reasons for poverty: laziness, sin or bad judgment. Often those who care for the poor are of the social left, which doesn't include many evangelicals.

* *Militarism*. During the Reagan years outspoken Christian leaders, usually from an evangelical church, pressed for military build-ups to reduce the Soviet threat

and to preserve the western world from atheistic communism. Fuelled by fear and the loathing of an inefficient communist system, it seemed appropriate to support a build-up of a military defence to protect the West against that system.

We forget Old Testament prophetic warnings that a nation is only as strong as its moral foundation. Militarism assumes that our values and heritage can only be preserved by military hardware. What it omits is the Bible message that God is a preserving God.

Should we spend our time and effort defending our evangelical message and heritage? I think not. The best defence is a strong offence. There is no greater testimony to the evangelical message of God's grace and truth than to live His life. While we admit our vulnerabilities and failings, the power of God's love, lived out in our lives, will be our best defence.

**The power of God's love
lived out in our lives
is our best defence**

10
Beware of the Grumpies
Is crankiness excusable?

A HIGHLY TOXIC pollutant is eroding the ozone layer of the Canadian spirit. Its official name is public debate. It could better be described as a case of the Canadian grumpies.

Listen to a radio phone-in show, switch on The Journal, scan your local newspaper or eavesdrop on the chatter at the neighbourhood coffee spot and what do you hear? Grumpy, nasty comments about anyone from politicians to labour leaders and anything from taxes to the weather.

Complaining, griping and whining seem to overpower rational discussion. This is apparent in such areas as the language debate, interprovincial relations, abortion, taxes, our relationship to the United States, immigration, the environment, fish quotas, prayer in public schools, western alienation, the federal deficit and bank interest – the list can go on and on.

Are Canadians naturally this way? Is it a national characteristic?

What do we make of Canadian historian J.M.S. Careless' analysis: "Americans cannot conceive of losing unless there's a conspiracy somewhere. Canadians, constrained by climate, distance, and history, see no reason to expect victory."

Every country faces tough times and tough choices. Canada, for most of its history, has experienced strong economic growth and a measure of peace and harmony.

So why this mood of the grumpies? I admit that from time to time there are serious divisions in our nation that cannot be ignored, humoured or camouflaged. We have many reasons to be concerned. But there is a difference between being concerned and sliding into a nasty, belligerent mood.

Review the list of complaints a few paragraphs back. Ask yourself, "Do I react to these issues in a way that's different because of my Christian world view? Does my attitude to language issues or taxes vary from that of my neighbour who makes no profession of faith in Christ?"

There's an old adage that says, "If Christ is Lord at all, He must be Lord of all." Thus nothing, including my attitudes to taxes or the language debate, escapes the lordship of Christ.

How we see life

Each of us sees life through a lens that is shaped and refined by our family, education and experience. That doesn't necessarily mean the lens is acceptable to Christ. His call is to see life through the lens of biblical faith.

Elisha the prophet and his servant were surrounded by the enemy army. The servant, anxious for the life of his master, cried out in despair. The old prophet simply prayed that his servant's eyes would be opened. The servant, now seeing through a different lens, saw beyond the immediate situation. And there was God's army.

How do I view this country and the people who share it with me? Through a lens that is different? When the grain prices change farming patterns, am I driven to despair? When the abortion debate leads to laws much less biblical than I had prayed for, do I conclude that God's creation has been forgotten? When immigrants jump the queue, do I lash out in anger? When taxes are too high, is my only interest the impact on my paycheque?

As I watch the evening news or read the daily paper, I would do well to view events through a biblical lens. This involves:

A view of the holy. Our purpose for living cannot be defined by the size of a fish quota or by the percentage of income devoted to mortgage payments. My life is an arena of the holy where God is active in purifying the quality and beauty of my life.

A view of the sacred. "Sacred" is used to give special importance to something. We call our Canadian health care system a "sacred trust." What I value most highly – because of its benefit to me – I call sacred. We've lost an understanding that the sacred is that which is ultimate, far beyond our self-centred interests.

A view of immanence. Simply put, immanence is a view of God that recognizes He is not only in control but is present in life. Thus the parliamentary agenda is not set without God's knowledge. Too often we act as if God is either unaware or unable to do anything.

A view of legacy. While reflecting on the past, we must keep peering into the future. Life is going somewhere; it is not pointless. What we do today has consequence. The sins of today's national debt will be passed on to our children. Good agricultural stewardship today will pay dividends in the future. God rewards and punishes. Ultimately Christ will wind up history into the new heaven and the new earth.

A view of God's creation. All peoples are his creation: a francophone in Sault Ste. Marie, an anglophone in Trois Rivieres, a Sikh in Burnaby, a Filipino in Winnipeg or a Native Indian in Kenora. Though divided by colour, race, religion and culture, all are loved by Jesus Christ.

A view of biblical justice. Evangelicals are trapped by a fear that we may lose our freedoms. Instead of reacting in fear let us live out the call of the Word to oversee and protect justice for others. Resist the human temptation of living to protect self, and discover the beauty and majesty of upholding God's justice for all.

Grumping and complaining tells others that our God is weak; that the world is out of control; that God is stumped by evil; that our efforts are fruitless.

Instead let's bring a different message into our conversation, a different emotional tone to our speech. "May the words of my mouth and the meditation of my heart be pleasing in your sight, O Lord, my Rock and my Redeemer."

**Nothing, including my attitudes
towards taxes or the language debate,
escapes the lordship of Christ.**

11
Watch Out for Wheelbarrows!

What you see is not always what you get

NIKITA KHRUSHCHEV LIKED to tell the story of a timberwork factory in Leningrad.

A wave of petty thefts had broken out at this factory and the Soviet government responded by placing a guard at each of the factory gates. One day a guard, who knew each worker, saw Pyotr Petrovich pushing out a wheelbarrow loaded with a suspicious-looking sack.

"What have you got there, Petrovich?" asked the guard.

"Just sawdust and shavings," was the reply.

"Come on," the guard said, "I wasn't born yesterday. Dump the sack out of the wheelbarrow."

Petrovich dumped out the contents and, sure enough, all there was in the sack was sawdust and shavings. Each night the same story was played out.

Finally after a week the guard's suspicion got the best of him.

"Petrovich," he challenged, "I know you're smuggling

something. Unless you tell me what it is, I won't let you out of here." Petrovich, knowing he was trapped, finally admitted, "Wheelbarrows, my friend, wheelbarrows."

As evangelicals we stand guard over biblical doctrines but allow the "wheelbarrows" of modernity or worldliness to slip by. We've rigorously opposed the infiltration of theological liberalism. At the same time, we've failed to notice the wheelbarrows of materialism. That's modernity: Christian values being determined by the surrounding culture.

A less obvious example is the growing evangelical preoccupation with church buildings. While a strong case can be made for building serviceable and attractive facilities, the values of our culture encourage us to believe that the building boom is evidence of God's blessing. Our agenda is being written, or at least influenced, by the world's material standards.

Riding the extremes
Early in this century conservative Protestants became preoccupied with the issues of Sunday observance and temperance (anti-drinking). They were concerned that worldly behaviour would encroach on the church. As a result, evangelicals were characterized as those who didn't smoke, drink, dance or attend movies. To ensure that the church did not accept the lifestyle of the world, each philosophy or practice coming into the church was scrutinized to make sure it didn't contain anything that would contaminate the faith.

The pendulum is swinging
Today, evangelicals are attempting to define spirituality in more positive terms, with less of an anti-behaviourial

emphasis. We want to be seen to stand for biblical truth without becoming preoccupied with the "don'ts" at the expense of the "do's."

Consider, for example, the issue of technology. As part of God's creation there is nothing worldly about it whatsoever. But overconfidence in it can lead to a worldly assumption – that technology is the way to reach our world. While it is *a* way to speak to large groups of people, to put our trust in technology is idolatry. Christ's model of becoming flesh and blood (the incarnation) and actively engaging our world in love is how the world will be won.

In the early 1970s, author and Christian apologist Os Guiness was asked by a sociology professor, "By the end of the 1970s who will be the worldliest Christians in America?" The professor quickly answered his own question. "I guarantee it will be the fundamentalists." Why? As a sociologist he knew how people recently emerging from a socially marginalized position would want what they had despised and seek approval from those who had ignored them. And so symbols of power, wealth and influence would be sought to achieve social legitimacy and a place at the trough of materialism.

Modernity, or worldliness, can rob us of the true heart of the gospel. Too easily, ministries and religious leaders, while holding to orthodox evangelical doctrines, can be overtaken by the combined lure of money and status, and by an idolatrous faith in technology. This, too, is modernity: the subtle takeover of our message by the materialistic values of the surrounding culture.

In North America the fastest-growing churches and those with the most modern resources and best buildings have tended to be evangelical. I rejoice in the evidence of creative planning and aggressive outreach. I have no wish for any group to resort to worn-out methodologies or facilities.

But I do find it curious that the recruiters for materialistically driven pyramid type sales organizations, which sell everything from soap to cosmetics, recruit a surprising number of people from these growing evangelical churches. Only a few years before, such activity was seen as worldliness.

At the same time, the church's interest in reaching out to the drug-infested community, the drunkards and the despised is diminishing. How many evangelical churches have we built in the inner cities in the past decade? With relentless regularity we escaped from the complexities of the inner cities. How many sermons have you heard recently about the needs of the poor and despised? Fostered by an aberrant theology which maintains that wealth is an evidence of God's blessing and that God's rewards are best measured by income, possessions and luxury holidays, we are pressured to buy into the assumptions of modernity.

Yes, modernity has caught up to us. The values of the modern world are becoming our values. The socially marginalized are pushed to the side in our desire to match the world, step by step, using the world's symbols of success.

Lopsided interests
Christians are deeply concerned, and rightly so, by the rapid declines of public ethical and moral values. But our determination to speak to issues such as abortion and pornography may produce gonging bells and tinkling symbols if we do not balance our public policy concerns with a deep commitment to love and care for those who are unlovely, unattractive, unable to help pay our church

mortgage, unaccustomed to our form of worship, and out of step with our style of church life.

Amos's call for justice cannot be dismissed as irrelevant simply because it is in the Old Testament. Let us hear his discomforting words.

"I despise your religious feasts . . . Away with the noise of your songs; I will not even listen to the music of your harps. But let justice roll on like a river, righteousness like a never-failing stream."

Worldliness is not the same as having attractive, efficient church plants. Neither is it the use of modern technology in ministry. Rather, it is embracing the world's standards of excellence and success as our own.

We rightly criticized mainline churches for the worldliness of their liberal theology. Too many of these churches caved in to the 20th-century forces of rationalism, liberalism, scientism and modernism. However, while we in the evangelical church have fought the battle for the Bible, screened doctrine to ensure an evangelical purity, and opposed unacceptable forms of social behaviour, we have been in danger of substituting modernity (worldliness) for godliness.

Though we have guarded ourselves from the extremes of liberalism, we have become susceptible to the subtle forms of worldliness: craving the symbols of wealth instead of loving the poor; lusting after political power instead of serving with a loving, sacrificial heart; seeking public acceptance instead of longing for the presence of God's Spirit; pouring our time and money into self-serving ministries and leaving out the fatherless families in our communities; channelling our anger only at the evil of abortion and ignoring the desperateness of those trapped by sin and failure.

Khrushchev's story is a prophetic word to us evangelicals: beware of those who scrutinize the sacks and miss the
wheelbarrows.

**We stand guard over
biblical doctrines
but allow the "wheelbarrows"
of modernity to slip by.**

12
Together We Stand

By cooperating under a national association, we can better affect Canada for Christ

ONE OF THE marks of the 20th-century evangelical move-ment has been fragmentation. Split among scores of denominations, agencies and missions, and ruled by a the-ology of the church which retains power in the local con-gregation, we are anything but centralized. Someone said that evangelicalism is free enterprise at its worst; we all do what's right in our own eyes.

Within our independence, however, an interdependence is very much at work. Although it seems we're driven out-ward by the centrifugal force of independence, the Spirit is the centripetal force which draws us together.

In 1846, the World Evangelical Alliance was formed. Today under the World Evangelical Fellowship, over 60 countries have national associations. Their common goal is to generate fellowship and a cooperative spirit.

As this force of evangelicalism rises (it's estimated there are two hundred million evangelicals in the world), two questions arise: What is an evangelical and why is it important to cooperate?

What does "evangelical" mean?

In the early 1500s a young priest, disturbed by what he saw in the church and struggling with his own salvation, initiated a religious movement known today as Protestantism.

Martin Luther, without intending to, left the Roman Catholic Church. Critics called those who followed him "protestants"; but Luther called them "evangelicals." Taking a New Testament word, "evangel," meaning "the good news," he formed a new Christian community. The word came to denote those who believe the Bible is God's Word and our final rule for faith, who rely totally on God's grace for our salvation, affirm the divinity of Jesus Christ and the work of God's Spirit in life. It came to mean other things, depending on culture and the time. But essentially it referred to non-Roman Catholics who based their life on God's Word.

Indeed, there existed a number of branches of the Christian church which eventually was called Protestantism. It included the high church and enthusiasts, state church and free church, reformed and Arminian. The evangelical view of the Bible continued as the main force of Protestantism up to the mid 1800s.

During the mid part of the 1800s, a new movement of rationalism shed a sceptic's light on the reliability of the Scripture. Doubt infiltrated the church system, beginning with its seminaries, first in Europe and then in North America. Theological liberalism became a major force which reshaped much of the Protestant church world-wide.

This liberalism split Protestants. To add insult to injury, evangelicals (sociologists refer to us as conservative Protestants) reacted and withdrew into an anti-intellectual, anti-society mood. Also events such as the Scopes "monkey trial" in the 1920s discredited many of those who believed that the Bible is indeed true and trustworthy.

Evangelicals and liberals waged a debate which lasted past the middle of the century. Over the past few decades, however, changes have been taking place within the evangelical community. Instead of ignoring social issues and concentrating only on matters of internal spirituality, evangelicals are changing and showing greater interest in the biblical call for justice and mercy.

Where are the evangelicals today?

During the 1950s and 1960s evangelicals were maturing – refining a more coherent theology, building better schools, training teachers, developing larger churches and becoming more involved in local and world social issues. They were losing their fear and slowly engaging more with the culture.

Beginning in the late 1960s, statistics began to show that mainline churches were losing their public influence. Their membership decreased. Often their preaching got caught up in social agendas, with less and less time for biblical exposition or the call for personal repentance.

The world learned of the spiritual legacy of Protestant liberalism. Its epitaph said it all: "God is dead."

Along with this theological flow, something else was changing: our society's moral foundation. Little did we know that following World War II, Christian faith to many would become only a faint memory. Although traditional evangelical churches began to grow (in some cases explode), the majority of the population remained either Catholic or mainline Protestant. And it seemed that for many Protestants, faith was more nostalgia than personal commitment. As more and more people moved away from personal faith, society became absorbed with freedoms, personal liberty and varying forms of relativistic morality.

Regardless of how you measure it, in moral terms there has been a decided decline in the quality of life over the past two decades. Even though evangelicals have tried to stick to their moral and theological guns, they still have had little presence or ability to influence the general direction of society.

Following the war, the World Council of Churches (WCC) was formed, along with the Canadian Council of Churches (CCC). The CCC, as the major Protestant coalescence, became the prime spokesgroup for Canadian Protestantism to government, society and media.

In the time of about 1960 to 1985, the evangelical community pushed out in all areas. And today in many places it's the worshipping majority. Recent Canadian studies note that, within the anglophone communities, on Sunday morning more evangelical Protestants are worshipping than are mainline Protestants.

The need for a public witness

Yet even given this growth, evangelicals are at best misunderstood and at worst ignored. This is a function of several factors: evangelical fragmentation and a high sense of independence; evangelical fear of getting involved in the world and losing their focus of anticipating the return of Jesus; and a failure among evangelicals to understand and implement the meaning of Christ's Kingdom.

Society at best has religious memories, but no vital,

dynamic personal accountability to Jesus and His church. Evangelicals have too often kept to themselves, preserving the blessings of faith, working on the false premise that the more I keep, the more I have. Jesus said reality is different: "Unless a kernel of wheat fall into the ground and dies, it remains only a single seed. But if it dies, it produces many seeds." God's Spirit is calling us to "Occupy till I come." His message is not, as some have assumed, "Build spiritual fallout shelters until I come"!

Building national evangelical groupings

We can learn some lessons from other nations. In 1846, the Evangelical Alliance was formed in England. Today over 60 countries have developed national evangelical fellowships. In the United States, the National Association of Evangelicals (NAE) since its founding in the late '40s, has been active in assisting its members in a number of ways. Dr. Carl F. H. Henry points to the formation and activity of NAE as being one of the most significant factors in the present impact of evangelicals in the U.S.

In Canada, geographical and linguistic fragmentation along with congregationalism and denominationalism separate us from each other. If we are to build strength in the face of declining church influence and the overpowering force of secularism, we need to find ways to get to know each other and work together.

With the religious pluralism, moral shift and rising governmental presence, evangelicals are realizing that no longer can we keep to ourselves, ignoring the government, societal values, or each other. If something is going to be done, it must be done together.

The value of a national association is to bring evangelical leaders together to foster understanding about who we are, to identify issues that concern us and to develop strategy on what we can do about them.

A national voice

We can also find ways, within the strength of our larger community, of being a voice to government, not in confrontation, but with a spirit to enable, encourage, and inform of our constituency and concerns.

We also believe it's vital we learn to speak to the broader culture via the secular media, clarifying, speaking out and debating those issues that affect our churches.

To accomplish these objectives we need to work together. Independently, many of our denominations would find it difficult to devise a strategy, for example, to interface with the CRTC on religious broadcasting, the Department of Justice on penal reform, the Department of Education on funding of private schools or the Supreme Court on interpreting religious freedom. But together we can pool our resources and speak with effectiveness and clarity.

Over the past few decades, as government went its merry way writing abortion, divorce and penal laws, opening the doors to all kinds of anti-Christian attitudes, the evangelical community became a preaching post rather than a voice. We drifted. We accepted governmental pronouncements uncritically, somehow believing it was God's will, or feeling there was nothing we could do to influence culture apart from church services.

Occupy till I come

What are our options? The first is to surrender. We continue on our present course, fragmented and divided, solely concerned with personal salvation.

Or we can allow Christ's reminder to work "Until I come back" to fill us with courage and faith so that our lives, churches and organizations will see the big picture, stop quibbling over differences and get on with the issues of the Kingdom.

Christ's call to work "until I come back" does not mean, "Build spiritual fallout shelters until I return!"

Part Two
CHRISTIANS AND
THE PUBLIC ARENA

13
Advancing Biblical Values in a Secular Society

The role of Christian faith in public issues

As I'M INVOLVED in debating various governmental proposals, I wonder, "What is the role of religious faith in solving public issues?" The question is crucial: how are we to advance our values in a nonbelieving society?

Christians face a very real problem in speaking to moral issues. Our basic assumptions about life are not shared by many of the prime influencers in our society.

It's important to understand, as we engage in various debates, that biblical morality no longer has the clout which was deemed best for our society by most Canadians during at least the first half of the 20th century.

Secularism
Why have we lost that basic consensus? Is it because so few Canadians believe in God or in the values expressed by the Bible?

No. Polls show that almost nine out of ten Canadians

61

believe in God. Sixty-six percent say they believe Jesus is the Christ.

The problem is the rising tide of secularism. As described in modern thought, secularism flows from two basic views. One, religious faith should have nothing to do with public life or, two, God is outside the scope of human understanding – he's either nonexistent or unavailable.

Many Christians accept the first view. They may believe in a personal God and the divinity of Jesus but they have been trapped into believing that faith is to be kept separate from any debate which forms public policy.

In effect, they are saying, "Continue to believe in your religious faith privately, but don't bring it into the community debate." Thus religion is seen as being private. If we use biblical arguments in writing public policy, most will protest saying, "Don't push your religion down our throats."

Pluralism

Alongside the dominant influence of secularism is pluralism; an acceptance of many beliefs and views. An underlying assumption of pluralism is that because there are many views, no one view is right. The previously assumed view – Judeo-Christianity – which underlies much of our public policy of the past, no longer rules. We must understand that while the rules of the game have been changed pluralism should not become a threat. For by its very nature it assures us a place at the table of debate and decision-making.

There is a danger. The prevailing influence of secularism may seek to override the rights pluralism offers and to suggest that because the group or the idea is religious, it has no place at the table. This idea must be challenged.

Our task

Should we then stop believing in our biblical views of life? Of course not. What is at stake, however, is how we go about engaging in the debate. Our task is to demonstrate the validity of our concerns and put forth ideas so that even those outside the household of faith will recognize their value and at least stop and listen.

Compromise?

We are in a very difficult situation. We're convinced that biblical truth is the final basis for our faith. Yet we live in a society that says choices will be based not on one world view but on many. Does it then mean we are forced to compromise?

Some say you compromise when you agree to work with others with whom you are in disagreement or whose standards fall short of yours.

The fact is, we're called to meet people part way. And doing so doesn't mean that values have been compromised. It's just that very few agree completely on any one thing. It takes willingness to work together on areas of agreement, all the while recognizing that although disagreements exist, it doesn't mean that either side has compromised.

Setting an agenda

Given that we no longer can expect others to agree with our conclusions, because they disagree with our premises, what are we to do in terms of influencing public policy?

Our arguments should appeal to common sense. For example, regarding pornography we argue that the exploitation of nudity and sexuality actually degrades human life. You don't need to quote Bible verses to prove that.

It's not our intention, as some might suggest, to impose our religious values on Canadians. We're not attempting to turn back the cultural clock. Neither are we calling for strict censorship.

Rather, we're simply asking for a reasoned understanding of the harm being brought to women, children and men. Even though our views will be considered by some as too narrow, we do ask from those who disagree with us that they accord us the dignity of listening to our concerns.

The same holds true for the abortion issue. Pro-choice advocates make it appear as if they're the only ones who care about the health of the mother. They attempt to cast us in the light of religious fanatics who glory in gruesome placards depicting the crime.

Yet they don't understand that although our concerns flow from a religious view of life, we aren't attempting to push our religion. Rather, we ask that they consider the medical reality of life existing in the early beginnings of a fetus. But instead of listening to this deep, inner cry, they push us to the other side of the street where too often the only thing we can do is carry our signs and sign our petitions.

It doesn't happen overnight

This slide in our nation's moral condition didn't happen in a year or two. It has been going on unchecked for years. And for us evangelicals, a little humility is in order. While secularism pressed its way into the minds of Canadians, we stayed in our comfortable, sectarian corners. As abortion reared its ugly head, we backed off, claiming it was a Roman Catholic issue.

The Apostle Peter put it this way: " . . . always be prepared to give an answer to everyone who asks you to give the reason for the hope that you have. But do this with gentleness and respect" (I Peter 3:15).

As we proceed in finding solutions to these critical issues, we should keep Peter's words in mind.

May the gentle presence of Jesus be evident in everything we say and do. Isaiah, looking ahead to Christ, said, "He will not shout or cry out, or raise his voice in the streets" (Isaiah 42:2).

I pray that our words and attitudes will reflect our ultimate trust in Jesus, the reigning King.

Our arguments
should appeal
to common sense.

14
The Gods Must Be Snoring
Sloppy thinking fertilizes myths

MYTHS CAN BE very satisfying. Typically sweeping general-
izations, they usually contain enough truth to be easily
believable. But ready acceptance of a "fact" put forth in a
myth eliminates the need to think very deeply or objec-
tively on the subject. Myths are also dangerous. Their
seductive simplicity leads to faulty conclusions and false
foundations for action.

Myths are created in two kinds of environments: when
there is too little information and when there is too much.
In pre-scientific days, in the vacuum of insufficient data,
thunder was thought of as the gods snoring. Today, with
the development of science and the view that science has
all the answers, many believe the myth that life sprang
into existence by random selection.

None of us are exempt from living with myths. As
sophisticated, educated thinkers we undoubtedly believe
we're too smart to be trapped by a myth; but myths are

subtle and we would do well to recognize several that distort our view of culture and, hence, how we act.

Myth # 1. Politicians can't be trusted. Over the past decade, the antics of various American and Canadian politicians have heightened a general distrust of politicians.

Because we expect the standards of our politicians to rise above society's standards, whenever we find moral failure, mistaken judgment or a character flaw, our disillusionment is intensified. The sweeping generalization that no politician can be trusted becomes a public myth. Not only is it untrue; it creates an environment of distrust, eroding the ability both of individuals and the collective government to lead.

Myth # 2: The broadening of human rights automatically means progress. The entrenchment of the Charter of Rights and Freedoms into the Canadian Constitution (1982) was considered to be the crowning achievement of Pierre Trudeau. Riding on the crest of the popular wave of human rights, the assumption was that anything written under the rubric of "human rights" was good for society.

Canada is blessed (at least by the standards of other nations) with a highly developed conscience which calls for citizens to afford others dignity and human worth. This we applaud.

The myth in the human rights agenda, however, is that whatever gives freedom to the individual is good for all. The flaw is the assumption that we live only as individuals. In the clamour for personal rights we forget that we don't live as an archipelago – a group of islands in a sea – but as people within communities. The collective rights of people within groups are apparently forgotten.

It may seem to be human, for example, to protect the identities of an AIDS victim's sexual partners. But at what point do we assert the rights of society to isolate and effectively quarantine a raging public disease?

Myth # 3. Bigger government is a sign of progress. The state, a biblically affirmed plan of organization, has radically changed in recent years. Historically it has been responsible for protecting its citizens from external attack and internal anarchy. In recent decades, the state has flowered into statism, a belief that government is responsible for our well-being from the cradle to the grave.

In essence, we have made the government a demigod. We've added a crushing weight to an institution that is incapable of serving society to the degree expected. The further tragedy is that we create a scapegoat that implicitly relieves us from the responsibilities of family, enterprise and community.

Myth # 4. Restricting pornography is retrogressive. Pierre Berton ridiculed the government for attempting to set limits on books, magazines and films depicting explicit sexual activities. Resorting to the myth of human rights, Berton and others championed the mistaken notion that progress may be achieved if society were to sanction almost any form of public sexual expression.

The myth inherent in this reasoning is that expressed sexuality (as long is it doesn't exploit children or physically harm women) is liberating, satisfying and healthy. The false assumption is that pornography is harmless, creative diversion or an encouragement to sexual enjoyment.

In fact, a consequence of pornography is increased sexual perversion. As well, it is not so much an issue of personal freedom as it is greed. It grosses billions of dollars in North America each year. How cleverly the myth of pornography's innocence is used by self-serving promoters.

Myth # 5. Abortion is a feminist issue. This myth, on first examination, is easy to support. After all, it's women who bear children. Reproductive choice, then, is the woman's right alone, assert radical feminist groups. Others suggest the opposite. Studies are showing that men have a significant influence in the choice of abortion. More than we realize, it is the pressure exerted by men that pushes women to chose abortions, even though that may run contrary to a woman's own preference.

Commonly held notions or frequently repeated assertions often call for careful scrutiny. They may be myths which can lead to other distortions of truth. Vigilance concerning common assumptions is not only essential for good legislation but for the development of one's mind.

And of all people, Christians are called to truth; we have a biblical responsibility to give thought to society's issues, to base our actions and speech on careful, intelligent and honest considerations of such matters.

Sloppy thinking is fertile field for myths. And sloppy thinking has no place in the life of a follower of King Jesus.

"Do not conform any longer to the pattern of this world, but be transformed by the renewing of your mind."

Tough words, but good advice.

We have made governments demigods.

15
Watch What's Flying

What is the overarching vision of Canada?

FLAGS CAN MAKE important statements. After the U.S. Supreme Court acquitted an American charged with burning the Stars and Stripes, President Bush announced he would attempt to make the desecration of the American flag a violation of the United States constitution.

In Canada in the early 1990s, Quebec's *Fleur-de-Lis* was trampled in Cornwall and the Maple Leaf was dragged around the streets of Montreal. In neither case was anyone charged with an offence. The Cornwall incident was replayed ad nauseam on Quebec television to the outcries of offended Quebec nationalists. But the desecration of the Maple Leaf was almost ignored in the rest of Canada. These are classic examples of where nationalism reigns and where it doesn't.

All of this came at a time when provincial and national leaders were agonizing through hours of haggling and deal-making on the Constitution. Meanwhile, Canadians pondering options, looked out over the precipice and wondered at the possible outcome.

A friend (an American now working in a mayor's office in a Canadian city), obviously frustrated by this process of constitutional tinkering, asked why there seemed to be no overarching vision of this country. The question came as no surprise. I too wondered.

Nationalism

Then I compared how flags are treated in the United States, Quebec and the rest of Canada. The quick and angry reaction by Quebecers and Americans to the treatment of their flags signalled the value these symbols have to each community.

The passion Quebecers have for the *Fleur-de-Lis* should alert Canadian anglophones to the deep emotions of the Quebecois towards their traditions, cultural patterns and language.

Ask the Quebecois what their flag means to them and you will more than likely learn the overarching vision that gives them their sense of identity. They seem to know who they are and what they want to become.

But the rest of Canada is floundering. Divided by the bickering of regions and provinces, the deep resentment of aboriginals to provincial and federal governments, and disagreement on issues ranging from abortion to taxes, we seem to have lost the central driving force that defines who we are as a nation and attracts people to loyalty and a willingness to sacrifice for the greater good.

When speaking at a conference in the United States, I was asked what is the unifying force in Canada. I concluded that Canadians are drawn together when threatened by our neighbour to the south. We then suddenly assert our "Canadianism" and stand together. We define ourselves by what we aren't rather than by what we are. In today's political realignment, "what-we-aren't" definitions will be too weak to hold peoples together.

We do know that nationalism out of control is dangerous. The American inclination to link God and country is not without its dangers. It can lead to legitimizing whatever the government does because the government is supposedly linked to God.

But never fear. Canadian nationalism hardly exists. Indeed, passion for our nation is so cool as to allow the nation's disintegration. And that situation prevails because there is no overarching vision of who and what we are.

So what does the evangelical community have to say about Canadian nationalism? For a Christian believer, is it important to have a strong, vibrant nation? I say, "yes."

A country provides a foundation from which a person makes decisions for eternity. We set the course for eternity by our decisions and values established here and now. Because a country, by its laws of freedom, allows or disallows its citizens to make those eternity-defining choices, the nation itself can be an enabler for right decisions.

God and nations

God uses nations in accomplishing his will. Egypt was part of God's plan in raising up another nation. God called Cyrus, king of Persia, His servant. A nation, like a family, is a means of God's will being worked out in the world.

A nation is also mandated to extend mercy and justice to its citizens: "For he is God's servant to do you good" (Romans 13:4). If a nation is weak it will not be able to assert justice. The laws of the jungle will then rule.

Out of this social-political construct called Canada, good has come to many. "Blessed is the nation whose God is the Lord" is not an idle comment. We indeed have been blessed, and in turn that blessing has flowed to others. It has been suggested that in this century the church in Canada is second only to that of New Zealand in per capita giving of personnel and money to Christian ministries worldwide. Canada has been a spiritual breadbasket for many.

Indeed, a strong nation can be a means of great blessing. A fragmented, regionally insulated country may continue to exist as a political entity, but it will be weak, with increased threat from the outside because of its internal weakness.

The late George Grant, a 20th-century Canadian philosopher and an evangelical, lamented the condition of Canada. He wrote, "[Diefenbaker's] inability to govern is linked with the inability of this country to be sovereign."

In *Lament for a Nation, the defeat of Canadian Nationalism*, Grant argues that Canada as a political reality is lost in the continentalism of North America. He held no hope for Canada to continue as a vibrant, political entity.

With respect, I believe Grant will be proved wrong. I continue to believe in an overarching vision of this nation – that Canada is a place where God's purposes are being worked out. I do not hold on to tradition for its own sake. God's will is what matters. And from what I see, Canada continues to be an instrument in His hand.

However, countries are not built just because someone has a good idea. It calls for deep and lasting commitment. Those who believe that all of life is God's, let us keep a high view of what he might accomplish through this unique and blessed nation called Canada.

We define ourselves
by what we aren't
rather than what we are.

16
Our "Sacred" Myths

Innocent ideas may be nothing more than popularized lies

GRANDFATHER DIED WHEN I was only four years old. My parents had told me, "He was ready to meet the Lord." My childish mind interpreted that to mean that at the exact moment he was "to go," he would be standing by the old wood stove, stripped of his clothes, waving good-bye. That was my myth: an understanding of life created by what I had heard and what I was able to understand.

We all have myths – fictions or halftruths that form part of our way of thinking. Sometimes they are our own, woven out of memories and personal experience. Or they come to us from a parent, friend, hero or culture.

Myths often begin quite innocently. One person thinks it's true, tells another and soon an entire group believes it. The myth becomes part of the belief structure of that group with no questioning as to its validity.

My myth of grandfather being "ready to meet the Lord" satisfied me for some time. As a myth, it was harmless, not giving rise to any real danger. Other myths are not.

Within our own Christian community we have embraced numerous myths without critically examining them. Here are a few.

Myth # 1. The church should have nothing to do with politics. This myth suggests that the church's only role is to speak about our relationship to God.

Like all popular myths, this one contains an element of truth. The Bible does not call the organized, denominational church to run the government. I wouldn't want any denomination in Canada to rule our land.

A danger here, however, is in concluding that because a church should not rule politically, neither should Christians be involved in politics. In fact, the church has everything to do with politics, for it is made up of the people of God. As members of the church of our Lord, we are called to bring His reign to all of life.

Myth # 2. Because Christ is coming soon, the events happening in this world are no business of ours. Pivotal to biblical faith is the expectation that at some moment in history, Jesus Christ will again intersect time and space and establish His ultimate and final reign. This is called "the purifying hope."

Unfortunately, especially during troubled times, we use this vital component of faith as a means of escape rather than engagement. Life and time, created by God, are pushed aside as if they don't matter.

We live on this planet by God's design and in living are being prepared for his final kingdom. Thus, what we do here and now is critical. Someone has said that during this life, we are writing the genetic code for eternity.

Myth # 3. AIDS is God's judgment on homosexuals.
Two factors have bolstered this myth. First, we believe that
homosexuality as a sexual practice is disallowed by
Scripture. We also recognize the high percentage of victims who are or have been practising homosexuals.

The danger of this myth is that we can too easily say,
"You deserve it."

But we know that heterosexuals – and tragically, even
young children and babies – also are increasingly affected
by the disease. AIDS is not a punishment to any one group
of people. Rather, it is a message to the world that
humankind cannot violate God's laws without repercus-
sions. That goes for heterosexuals as well as homosexuals.

Myth # 4. You can't legislate morality. This myth has
been popularized both inside and outside of the church.
Look at any piece of legislation and you'll see moral principles which underlie its objectives. It's impossible for any
person or group to propose laws without having a view of
life, and that includes a view of morality.

You can't legislate spirituality or righteousness. These
are functions of God's Spirit at work. But morality is
expressed in the way we see people living and working
together.

The real question is: Whose morality are we legislating?

Critics have accused us of "trying to jam your morality
down the throats of nonbelievers." It is not our wish nor
design to force people to believe the gospel. We know that
won't work; moreover, it is contrary to the very nature of
God's grace and salvation.

However, if we back off and let those guided by secular-
ist views write the legislation, what we've done is to let
their moral views dominate.

Not only is it our right as Canadians to advance our views of morality in the writing of legislation, it is our Christian duty to persuade people of what we believe is true. This doesn't mean we force it or become obnoxious, but we are called to debate in the public forums of the land. And that's more scary than living with our myths.

Myth # 5. "Conservatism" is next to godliness. Evangelical Protestants are conservative in their theology as compared to the liberalism which has influenced much of mainline Protestantism this century. Often this inclination to interpret life out of a conservative framework can trap us into believing that any analysis that is "conservative" is true. "Conservatism," like any other ideology, replaces fidelity to the gospel and devotion to Jesus Christ. It prevents us from hearing the voice of God.

Jonah is a good example. He got angry when God accepted the repentance of the people of Ninevah. Jonah's stunted view of God's grace did not allow him to understand that his God could care for any people beyond his own, especially the notoriously evil Ninevites. Jonah was trapped by the myth of interpreting God's concern only out of his bias.

The Word has a way of exploding myths that keep us from seeing the truth of God's love for people everywhere.

Watch out for myths. Critically examine each "easy truth" in the full light of God's revelation. Myths limit life. Better to explode myths today than live with lies for a lifetime.

**We are called
to debate in the
public forums of our land.**

17
Beyond Civil Disobedience

Actions of civil disobedience can lead to new laws if supported by a sizable majority

CIVIL DISOBEDIENCE CAN seem conflicting for the Christian. Even strong pro-life supporters cringe when they see on TV a protester being forcibly dragged away from an abortuary by the police. The discomfort may not be so much their concern for the safety of the protesters as the realization that they're disobeying the law.

That is understandable. Pro-lifers tend to be religiously conservative people who have a high view of the law. They view obeying the law as fundamental to their responsibilities as a citizen. So when they see those involved in such tactics deliberately violating the law – even though they agree that a law prohibiting abortion is needed – their response may be, "But they have no right to disobey the law."

The problem for most of us when it comes to law-breaking to protect the lives of the unborn, is that our discussion is very emotional. Listen to a conversation about civil disobedience and one might hear: "I could never do that," or "If I did that I might lose my job," or "While I disagree with abortion, we must work through the right channels."

Before we either discount, reject or accept what is being done, consider this: While you may not like the approach of some who break the law by non-violent protest, what they are doing, in my opinion, is consistent with the practice of civil disobedience in a democratic system. For example, North American Indian tribes have refused to obey a court's injunction and by so doing have forced the government to negotiate.

Changing the law

And how can we forget what Henry Morgentaler did in Canada? He deliberately violated Section 251 of the Criminal Code. His objective? To force the courts to lay charges so the law would be tested in court. He believed the law was wrong and so he did what any Canadian can do – disobey a law one believes to be wrong in order for it to be examined. Morgentaler paid for his civil disobedience with heavy legal costs and by going to jail. While I don't agree with the case's outcome, and continue to believe that his lawyer manipulated the choosing of the jury, it was a procedure he was entitled to.

Martin Luther King Jr. did the same. He believed that the laws of the United States, as they related to civil rights, were wrong. And so he led a religious, passive form of civil disobedience. The story is well known. He is one of the heroes of the western world because he was willing to undergo discomfort, misunderstanding and opposition as he stood up for what he believed was morally right.

Those in Operation Rescue (the civil disobedience group which physically blocked entrances to abortion clinics in Canada and the U.S.) are operating in the same western tradition. They are willing to disobey court injunctions, believing their concerns are worth fighting for.

One may not like what is being done. But one should at least allow them the right to do what we have long treasured in our democratic world – the right of people to disobey laws they believe are wrong. Out of these forms of disobedience can come new laws.

Public disobedience
There are two other sides which those leading the protest must keep in mind.

This form of public disobedience surely highlights the issue and forces our public leaders to change their timeline in dealing with a public issue. But those leading civil disobedience may be in no position to participate in the writing of laws. Their public aggravation of leaders, and I'm sure the angering of many private citizens, will make it difficult for them to be part of the teams needed to draft laws and write policies. It will require others to lead the way in writing new laws.

Often those who are willing to subject themselves to public humiliation and physical imprisonment believe that because of the price they have paid they should be the ones who lead during the next stage. There is also the danger that they may see others who have not been part of the civil disobedience as either having compromised their beliefs or lacking courage.

It's important that they recognize, in the long term, the need to work with those who have other skills. Though I stand behind their right to practise civil disobedience, I plead with them to support long-term strategy and not just an immediate protest.

To convince a national government to pass a certain law, it must be supported by a significant majority. And if the majority does not support that proposed law, effort must be made to convince them. So the question to ask is, Will the action of civil disobedience help win over at least a sizeable majority who will support a government law?

Governments usually will do everything they can to avoid a controversial issue. They will only move when the public turns up the heat. Civil disobedience is one such fire.

Those who practise
civil disobedience
must see beyond
the immediate.

18
A Necessary Defence!

Alerting evangelicals to courts interpreting the Charter

FEW AFTER-DINNER conversations end up in a debate on the impact of the Canadian Charter of Rights and Freedoms on our lives. However, while moral/ethical issues such as abortion and pornography may dominate discussions of national concern, the court battles over "what the Charter really means" may be, in fact, one of the most important issues we face. Recent incidents demonstrate that evangelicals must take seriously the impact of court rulings and the consequent interpretation of what the Charter will mean in life.

The Charter: Background
The Charter of Rights and Freedoms was signed into law by Prime Minister Pierre Trudeau and Queen Elizabeth. Until then our courts were subject to the supremacy of Parliament. The elected legislators were the ultimate arbiters and protectors of individual rights and freedoms,

apart from those areas which had been given over to the provinces to manage. The courts ensured that the requirements of our old Constitution were adhered to, but Parliament was responsible for setting the rules.

Today we have a Charter, a written guarantee of individual rights and freedoms. This means that a person may challenge any legislation or governmental action by claiming that his or her rights under the Charter have been violated. The courts now have the final voice.

In this way we are increasingly like the United States. Often we hear U.S. citizens claim that their constitutional rights have been violated. In Canada, we are now able to do the same.

The Charter does two things: it provides written constitutional protection of individual rights and freedoms, and it establishes that the principle of sovereignty is subject to the primacy of the Constitution. All law, even if validly enacted by the Parliament or a legislature, is subject to review by the courts. The courts now have the final say, not Parliament. That's the shift!

The Charter is filled with high and lofty sounding words and ideas. But the precise meaning is unclear until decisions by the court actually shape the ideas contained in the Charter. For example, "freedom of religion" is an idea we all applaud. But what does the idea mean in reality? We don't know until a court clarifies it in a specific case.

How the Charter works

Defining what the Charter means is not unlike making jelly. The jelly ingredients come in the form of powder. To make it into "jelly" you need hot water and a mold. The jelly remains in powder form until mixed with hot water. Even then, it has no shape until it is poured into a mold.

Similarly, the Charter contains all the ingredients to make law, but until the components have been mixed in an actual case and shaped by a court decision, it remains simply an idea.

When a Charter idea, such as "freedom of religion" (the jelly powder) is mixed into an actual case of Canadian life (the hot water), the court is called to make a decision on what those words mean (pouring the mixture into a mold).

That's why cases that refer to issues like religious education in public schools are so vital. They become molds that define what "freedom of religion" means in the Charter. Once a decision is made those cases become part of the legal history of this nation. It develops a legal momentum. And as that momentum builds through subsequent court decisions, it will be almost impossible to reverse it.

The subtle effect of legal challenges is to shape our culture within a secular framework by the use of the Charter. Our objection is that to say religion must be excluded from public life is to say that the cultural mindset will be secular and humanistic – which itself is a religious world view.

The court and evangelicals

But is the court a place for evangelicals? Lawyer Peter Jervis puts it this way: "The process of constitutional litigation is a dynamic and formative process. Judges must interpret our new constitution and apply it to existing laws.

"This process requires judges to pour meaning into empty or vague constitutional phraseology, often without the assistance of previous judgments. If Christians desire the development of the constitution in a manner consistent with their values and world view, they must shed their reluctance or condescension for the legal process and become active participants."

Some time ago a court ruled that Bible readings and prayers in schools be disallowed because they violated the Charter. Evangelicals cried out against this decision. But when the court had heard the case, not one Christian group had taken time or shown any interest in intervening. On this vital issue there were none to defend the Judeo-Christian values and heritage of this nation.

The evangelical community must wake up! Instead of resorting to anger when we see the erosion of Christian values, why not give some time to constructive action or put up a few dollars to defend our values? Too often we protest, "That's none of our business." Or we pass it off by reminding each other of the new building or air conditioning sucking up available dollars.

We are coming to a point in our history when we may have to decide between paving a parking lot or defending Christian liberty.

We are coming to a point in our history when we may have to decide between paving a parking lot or defending Christian liberty.

19
To Win or Lose?

A scorecard faith blinds us from the true wins and losses

"WHAT WILL YOU do if you lose?" I was asked as I left the courtroom where we were opposing the Canadian Civil Liberties Association's attempt to remove religious instruction from public schools.

An interesting question; but one that assumes the only reason Christians engage in important public and social issues is to "win." The flaw in that argument is that we assume we can determine what is "winning" or "losing."

For example, what should be our response when we lose a court case on the place of religious education in the curriculum of the public schools? How should we react as most provincial governments allow Sunday shopping? Or what is to be our reply to an abortion bill which is seen by some as a loss for the pro-life side? Are we to consider these as wins or losses?

Some have candidly said, "If we can't influence legislation or legal decisions, then we should bow out." In plain language – if you can't win the battle, then get out of the war.

Basic to this way of thinking is that we engage in the battle with the assumption that winning is the only reason we are there.

What is winning?

I admit that has been my tendency. As a sports enthusiast I have never played just to enjoy the game. I play to win. But just because that's a reflection of my personality it doesn't mean that's how God calls me to think and act.

Here's the problem: If one assumes winning is the prime criteria for action, what I consider to be a win may, in Christ's view, be considered a loss.

A classic example is the issue of prayers and Bible readings in the schools. If the courts had permitted them to continue, it might have been seen as a "win." But, indeed, would it have been? Could it in fact have been a "loss"? If we had "won" it might have extended the false assurance that students are being nurtured by the gospel, thus absolving us from finding new and creative ways of touching students with a substantive gospel witness.

Now, having "lost" on the issue, we realize we no longer can pretend. The alarming state of affairs in our schools has awakened us to the harsh reality: we are raising a generation of young people who are, to a large extent, biblically illiterate. And we are forced to admit that an occasional brief Bible reading did little to break that cycle of illiteracy.

The Bible reminds us we see through a glass darkly. It's impossible for us to see ultimate consequences out of current "wins" or "losses." Eclipsed from our view are other movements which may later affect the issue.

Pop psychology

During the 1970s there was a surge of books, tapes and lectures on winning. The Psychology of Winning, a popular series of tapes by Gary Waitley, was designed to produce "winners." Our western economic system is built on the notion that with enough ingenuity and hard work you can be a financial winner. The free enterprise system assumes that financial rewards should go to those who risk and accomplish. Robert Schuller, minister of the Crystal Cathedral in California, has built his ministry on what he calls "possibility thinking."

Our culture has been steeped in this notion of "winning." But does it line up with what the Bible says about keeping score?

Hebrews chapter 11 begins with a listing of those who "won." But it doesn't stop there. It ends with a list of those who, while losing, actually won:

"Others were tortured and refused to be released, so that they might gain a better resurrection. Some faced jeers and flogging, while still others were chained and put in prison. They were stoned; they were sawed in two; they were put to death by the sword. They went about in sheepskins and goatskins, destitute, persecuted and mistreated – the world was not worthy of them. They wandered in deserts and mountains, and in caves and holes in the ground. These were all commended for their faith, yet none of them received what had been promised. God had planned something better for us so that only together with us would they be made perfect" (Hebrews 11:35-40).

The disciples, hidden away for fear of the authorities, believed that Jesus had lost. It took the coming of the Holy Spirit on the day of Pentecost to convince them that although Jesus had "lost" in the eyes of the world, He had actually won. The disciples' scorecard before Pentecost showed a loss; in reality Christ was in the heat of battle defeating Satan.

Paul could have considered his imprisonment as a loss to Roman injustice. Instead he saw the bigger picture. By using his Roman citizenship he was referred to Rome. There, although in prison, he was an instrument of grace. Some would have considered his situation as being a loss. He knew differently.

So how should we view our battles in the modern arena? Does it not matter that we make every attempt to influence politicians for a law protecting the unborn? Does it mean we back away from protecting religious education in the courts? No! There is nothing spiritual about fear, a lack of preparedness or a weak-hearted attempt to make a strong case in court. But it calls us to see our role differently than we would through the lenses of the world.

What is the common thread that weaves its way through the stories of Hebrews 11? What was absolutely essential to the ministry and life of Christ? It was faithfulness in living out a life of biblical truth and integrity. The so-called results were left for God to compute and post.

God does not call us to keep a scorecard. Neither does He supply us with an instant replay screen. Certainly, each play is entered into the vast storage capacity of God's infinite and eternal wisdom. But that doesn't give us the right to interpret the results. That's why the win-loss mentality of this age is faulty and misleading.

A scorecard mentality assumes that God is not in control. It implies that we can't leave the computing to His care; that our ways are His ways. God doesn't go out of His way to fool us. It's just that our minds are cloistered by our fallenness and by the time factor.

Our criteria

So what should we avoid as we establish the criteria for action?

1. Don't set the criteria out of the collective wisdom of your friends. Too easily we assume that our associates' point of view is God's. Because we often surround ourselves with those who think as we do, absent are contrary views which will help us see how trapped we are by our own biases.

2. Don't set the criteria for winning or losing according to what you like. We all understandably avoid pain. But that avoidance does not mean that the action resulting from that avoidance is supported by God's criteria for action.

3. Avoid setting your criteria by your political or nationalistic interests. If a particular governmental bill does not pass, and you think it should, does it mean that God's agenda for the country is destroyed?

4. Resist setting your criteria according to the latest theory on the return of Christ. We have lived in the last days since Christ ascended and will continue to do so until he returns.

Winning or losing is not the issue. Faithfulness is.

**Although Jesus had lost
in the eyes of the world,
he had actually won.**

20
Jesus a Socialist?

Human labels don't compute into the Godhead

ISN'T JESUS A SOCIALIST? a friend asked. Maybe he's a liberal, or perhaps a conservative, I offered.

Words are a marvellous means of saying what I mean and meaning what I say. But sometimes they get muddied.

That's why it's risky to insist that Jesus, the Bible or the church be defined in terms of any one view on the political/social spectrum. To do so not only confuses the meaning of the words; it also traps one into a corner where Christ is forced into a straitjacket of human ideologies, be they liberal, conservative or socialist.

So back to the question: Was Jesus a socialist?

It all depends. To my friend the word "socialist" suggests someone who cares for others, isn't greedy, attempts to distribute wealth more fairly and supports the rights of others. On the other hand, to her a conservative is one who is narrow in thinking, espouses free-enterprise capitalism (i.e., the rich are unfairly making money off the poor and vulnerable), and wants to impose rigid standards without caring for the truly weak. Liberals, to her, probably fit somewhere in between.

A little history

To make sense of what these terms mean, consider briefly how they have come to be used in the past few hundred years.

The slogan of the French Revolution was "Liberty, Fraternity and Equality." Liberalism is the child of that movement. The state was defined as an association for the protection of the individual. Liberalism viewed society as that which was to centre around freedom of the individual.

Conservatism sought to counter the liberal notion of the autonomous or free individual. Instead it emphasized the concept of community. It also attempted to slow down the rapid pace of change and conserve the values and traditions of the past.

Socialism, within the past 150 years, has come to mean people living and working together in a collective form and for the collective good. (Communism attempted to wed socialism with Marxism.) The state is to establish and maintain the collective forms of life.

Our problem is that these words have come to mean different things. For example, a United States president, running on a conservative platform, would be known in Europe as a liberal because those life views are based on the ideals of individualism. Yet in North America such political ideology would be termed conservative.

Three words

Today, in North America, these three words may best be understood this way:

Conservatism: "Hold on; don't change so fast; save our heritage. Reward initiative and let the financial marketplace operate."

Liberalism: "Fight for the rights of the individual. Use the power of government to rule the marketplace."

Socialism: "The state has the responsibility by central planning to ensure that goods and services are equally distributed."

You will quickly recognize that these definitions are too narrow. Also, in politics none of the three ideas is exclusive. A conservative government will readily use the heavy hand of government-regulated high interest rates to interfere in financial markets to accomplish its goals.

In the Soviet Union, those who stand opposed to the liberalization of the economic and political systems are called conservatives. The drive to institute a free-enterprise type of market is called liberalism. Yet in the West, that very same free-enterprise capitalism comes from a conservative political/economic ideology. Christians, therefore, should be careful to identify the context of usage of these terms. From time to time, our own heritage espouses all three.

Socialism: The notion of caring for others in a community setting has been practised by many Christians, including various Mennonite orders.

Conservatism: The Bible has much to say about preserving the values and heritage that come down to us from godly parents.

Liberalism: Old Testament prophets called on God's people to extend justice and mercy to individuals.

Confusion over words

The confusion over these labels arises, in part, from the fact that they all essentially describe political, economic and social theories and systems that are humanistic; none of them ultimately sees God as Creator and Saviour. In effect, each is secular. God is not part of their structure of meaning. Indeed, as you listen to the promotion of any of these ideologies, you can hear a heart beating with the belief that the ideology alone is the saviour.

So what is Jesus? He doesn't fit into any of our definitions or categories, be they clear or muddied.

A powerful statement of Christ's rising above narrow definitions comes from a letter to Diognetus written during the second century AD.

"The Christians are distinguished from other men neither by country or language, nor the customs which they observe . . . As citizens, they share in all things with others, and yet endure all things as if foreigners . . . They are in the flesh, but they do not live after the flesh . . . They obey the prescribed laws, and at the same time surpass the laws by their own lives. They love all men, and are persecuted by all . . . They are poor, yet make many rich."

Canadians don't need Christ's followers to flog any one of a number of human-centred and self-serving ideologies. Instead, let us allow the God who has become flesh to live out through us that which limited human equations cannot compute.

Jesus a socialist? Not from what I've seen of socialism – or conservatism or liberalism, for that matter.

From time to time
Christian tradition
has espoused all three –
socialism, conservatism and liberalism.

21
A "Christian" Party?

Is political power a legitimate means to advance the cause of Christ?

IN RECENT YEARS there has been renewed interest in the development of a "Christian" political party. I understand the frustration that pushes many to consider establishing such a party. Conservative Protestants have assumed that a conservative type of government would affirm and advance biblical values.

We know that to consider political and economic conservatism to be synonymous with theological conservatism is not only to be naive but misled. Any mainstream political party today is forced to operate in the current mix of pluralism. Although we are often reminded of the biblical influence that has shaped much of our Canadian culture, political parties are structured on the premise of secularity.

Before one answers the question of the desirability of having a "Christian" political party, we must ask, How can the followers of Jesus Christ best operate in today's political, social and moral environment?

Guidelines

I offer the following guidelines for our thinking.

Nothing is outside of God's ownership. "The earth is the Lord's and everything in it . . ." (Psalms 24:1). We are his instruments of grace. God uses people; be it shepherds to witness Christ's coming or Pharaoh to prepare his people in Egypt.

Power is legitimate. Just because power may, and too often does, corrupt, it doesn't follow that power itself is corrupt. "For there is no authority except that which God has established" (Romans 13:1).

Society is shaped by ideas, both for evil and good. Galileo forced a rethinking of space and the sun's relationship to our planetary system.

People in leadership form society by creating structures, laws and programs which influence the way people believe and live.

Given these underlying assumptions, how does Canada work?

From our beginnings we have forged a country built on the "mosaic" rather than "melting-pot" pattern of the U.S. Today that pattern continues. Now we call it multiculturalism.

Out of that has emerged the notion of pluralism – that each group has a right to its own views, its own culture. This leads to an accepted understanding that no one group has exclusive ownership of either what is true or best. That makes it difficult for Bible believers, but nevertheless, it's the way our country is structured and how it operates.

I disagree with those who assert that faith and politics shouldn't mix. Politics is the way we govern. And because ruling is God's business it is therefore also mine. John

Calvin called it "the cultural imperative": the responsibility of Christians to work for righteousness in government.

Laws are not neutral. Morality is legislated. Every law is built on a view of life. As well, a society is not static but always changing. To avoid politics is not to be holy but smug. "I'll not dirty my hands" is not being courageous but weak. It's a cop-out.

Dangers

So what about a specifically "Christian" party?

Charles Colson, former advisor to President Nixon, suggests there are three dangers to thinking that by taking over political control we will solve the problems of the world.

First, people who believe so will become more cynical as problems increase. Not only will they become alienated from leadership but conclude that good people can do nothing.

Second, false security will take over. "We'll elect our kind of people (even evangelicals) and then everything will be okay." Colson reminds us; "The Kingdom of God will not arrive on Air Force One."

Third, we can be trapped into believing that by gaining power we advance the cause of Christ. Jesus reflected on that to Pilate: "My kingdom is not of this world. If it were, my servants would fight to prevent my arrest . . . " (John 18:36).

There is a fine line of distinction here. We are called to be "in" this world – to assert King Jesus' lordship – yet not "of" this world – trapped by the false notion that human political systems can and will solve all problems.

A "Christian" party assumes by its very construct that it has all the answers. And whenever it fails – and it will –

the Christian community (and in this case, evangelicals) will get blamed for its failures.

A party that makes its platform exclusively "Christian" will be hampered by restricting membership, preventing it from becoming a significant political force. It may also ghettoize Christians, keeping them from influence in the mainstream parties.

Nineteenth-century philosopher Friedrich Nietzsche, whose writings became foundational to Hitler's Nazism, said, "Be careful when you fight dragons lest you become a dragon."

The Psalmist warned us about idols: "Those who make them will become like them, and so will all who trust in them in them" (Psalms 115:8).

**"The Kingdom of God
will not arrive
on Air Force One."**

22
Lies Snowball

Governments, in misrepresenting truth, wreak havoc

WE CHUCKLE OVER the absurdity of those who believe the world is flat. Yet, ludicrous as it may seem, many still refuse to accept the historical reality of the Holocaust.

In the mid 1940s, the world woke up to the Nazis' "final solution" of European Jews. Today some still try to dispute that dark moment, claiming it never really happened. Publications continue to promote hate through literature suggesting that history's record of the annihilation of six million Jews is a hoax. Absurd as these allegations are, they are more than just intellectual dishonesty or blatant racism. They demonstrate a spreading problem of citizens who are willing to believe they've been sold a lie.

I have wondered why some still try to deny what Jews worldwide cause us to remember each year – the Holocaust. The growing anti-Jewish feeling around the world sometimes is subtle. But even the use of humour can't hide the bitter reality: it's racism.

Vietnam

I gained a new understanding of the vulnerability of people to believe in a lie in an examination of the Vietnam war. I discovered a partial answer to the question of why people will choose to believe an obvious lie when faced with photos and films verifying the Nazi death camps.

A TV special on Vietnam took us back to the Gulf of Tonkin Resolution of August 5, 1964. Lyndon Johnson was president. He had told the world the U.S. would not launch an air strike on North Vietnam. Then a report, the one President Johnson believed, said that two U.S. destroyers were being attacked by North Vietnam torpedo boats. Another report was that the radar on the U.S. ships had made a mistake. What had been reported as torpedo boats was, in fact, a storm. A U.S. fighter pilot warned the Pentagon not to respond. He said he had not been able to verify the existence of any enemy presence in the Gulf of Tonkin. Johnson chose to ignore these warnings and proceeded to launch a massive air strike against Hanoi. This became the turning point of the war. Not only did the war escalate into one of the bloodiest the United States has ever fought, but it plunged many into a well of distrust, one from which many have not yet climbed.

Here is the point. As a government seems to misrepresent truth to its people, it makes it almost impossible for anyone to detect the lie. When someone questions the leader, the one doing the questioning is discredited by appearing to be unpatriotic.

But on the Vietnam issue, the unexpected happened. A large number of Americans rose in protest, not only over what they believed was an illegitimate and immoral war, but over what they felt was a series of calculated lies concocted by their government. At first it seemed that only social radicals – those with long hair and guitars – protested. But then the protests spread. Soon Sunday School teachers joined in. The tragedy is that they began to distrust their own president. Not only did they distrust their government, but they also assumed that when the government made a claim, the opposite would probably be true. The fudging by government of truth produces a citizenry which will on other issues resist overwhelming evidence and choose instead to believe a lie.

Dr. Scott Peck, psychiatrist and author, became a committed Christian when he admitted there was a reality called evil. In his book *People of the Lie* (Simon and Schuster, 1983), he says: "The poor in spirit do not commit evil. EVIL is not committed by people who feel uncertain about their righteousness, who question their own motives, who worry about betraying themselves. The evil in this world is committed by the spiritual fat cats, by the Pharisees of our own day, the self-righteous who think they are without sin because they are unwilling to suffer the discomfort of significant self-examination." (p. 72)

This was reinforced by a conversation I had with Floyd McClung, who began a Youth With A Mission ministry to prostitutes in Amsterdam. He said prostitutes are very clear about who they are and don't deceive themselves about their identity. It shouldn't surprise us that Jesus so quickly forgave the sins of prostitutes and yet was devastating in his condemnation of the so-called religious leaders. For often it's the religious who hide under a lie of propriety, pretending to be who they aren't.

Deception snowballs

The magnitude of a governmental deception is such that it becomes almost irrefutable. And it seems the bigger and more preposterous the lie, the more it takes on a cloak of honesty. The ultimate loss, however, is that people not only begin to distrust what government, big business, media or large institutions say, but they also fall prey to those who contradict the accepted ideas, on the basis that the smaller the voice, the more believable it is – even if in fact what it says is a lie.

Thus for those who attempt to discredit the history of Jewish death camps, they are aided by the distrust of what government, media or institutions have to say.

Without a doubt, the "gut" feeling of a large number of Americans was that the Vietnam debacle was not only devious and without legitimate national interest, but a cover up: a lie.

Jesus, it seems, can more easily reach the heart of a prostitute, who even though trapped by sin has not covered herself with self-deception. The tough nut to crack is a lie which has been layered by religious, national or institutional self-interest.

Even as Christ has called us to honesty, let us not stop-short of reminding leaders, regardless of political stripe, religious communion or institution, that they should trust us with honesty. Beware of the snowball effect dishonesty sets in motion. When the public believes they have been deceived, it's like sowing the wind and reaping a whirlwind (Hosea 8:7).

**The tough nut to crack
is a lie layered by religious,
national or institutional
self-interest.**

23
Communism Goes Kerplunk

In the mad rush to the West, is one form of materialism being replaced by another?

IN HISTORICAL TERMS it didn't taken long for Marxist-Leninist communism to hit the skids. Beginning with the writings of Karl Marx and the subsequent revolutions in the Soviet Union, communism wove its strands and secured its web over eastern Europe, China, parts of Indo-China, Latin America and Africa.

That web has now come apart. The force of human reaction to the brutal forms of communistic totalitarianism and the unbelievable inefficiencies of its economic theories have pushed open the gates of eastern Europe. While Gorbachev's *perestroika* and *glasnost* turned the key, the real force was people who refused to be denied their freedoms.

For too long millions marched silently to the gulag, quietly caving in to ruthless repression. For too long they lined up silently in shop queues, waiting as serfs, looking for basics to sustain human existence. For too long many silently practised their religious faith within the fellowship of underground churches.

For too long they silently obeyed the privileged few of bureaucracies who, while enjoying their holidays at the seashore, flogged the rhetoric of comradeship. For too long they silently sent their sons off to war, numbed by the party line that freedom groups of other nations needed their support.

The eerie cacophony of silence went on too long. It had to change. The human spirit will be silenced only for a time and then, regardless of the consequences, it must speak out. The volume became deafening.

Changing of the guards

Shortly after taking power, Gorbachev let it be known that the old Breshnev era was over. A new breeze would be allowed to blow through the country. He allowed more openness in the process; elections were held, allowing for political dissent. A limited form of free enterprise was tolerated. Then, to the surprise of everyone, he announced that countries of the Warsaw Pact would be free to choose their own political and economic structures.

As the walls of political encasement tumbled and the barbed wires of east/west lines were cut into pieces, tens upon tens of thousands voted with their feet, escaping to what they hope is the promised land of the West.

After more than 70 years the product of 20th-century communism was evident. It produced no real socialism in which people of a society were able to play on a level field.

Neither did 20th-century communism produce freedom. Pol Pot and the Khmer Rouge in Cambodia demonstrate a frightful lesson in the repression which often characterizes communism. It did not allow a true movement of the people; instead it limited freedom to a one-party system. Freedom to think was outlawed by Mao's form of communism both during the period of the Red Guards and as symbolized by the killings in Tiananmen Square.

Over the decades of this century communism has failed politically, economically, militarily and ideologically. Why is that?

Is it because it has been anti-democratic? Or is it due to its anti-western mindset? Some claim it was because modern communication showed the repressed millions what life is like in the western world. Others believe it was its anti-capitalistic nature which triggered its downfall. Undoubtedly all the above have contributed.

But at the core of Marx's writing was the ideology of materialism. In brief, it viewed the world as divided between the bourgeois and workers; out of the tension a truly classless society would emerge. Completely ignored was the nature of creation, for in Marxism, atheism reigns. Thus, with no God there is no essential spirituality; life is determined by materialism. That, in my view, is its Achilles' heel: the theory is based not on socialism but materialism.

Western democracy, rising from the soil of European Christianity, has held to the primacy of individuals within community seeking freedom and justice. It has lived in tension with materialism. But what held materialism in check was a Judeo-Christian view of humankind. Due to the encroaching presence of secularism that tension of holding materialistically driven society in balance is being lost.

In the West we are quickly moving down the road of secular democratic materialism. Secularism pushes out of our economic considerations a view of humankind which sees people as spiritual beings. As this spiritual understanding is elbowed to the sidelines of cultural life, materialism, steeped in a secular view of the world, becomes the central ideology, just as in communism.

What's the difference?

So how does atheistic communistic materialism differ from western secular democratic materialism? At the moment there is a difference because of the pervasive presence, in most democracies, of a Judeo-Christian understanding of life. But as that diminishes the western form will be dictated by materialism. And then what will we have to offer?

While communism's materialistic idol has led to repressive totalitarianism, the West's idol of materialism may lead to narcissistic anarchism in which self-centredness rules.

As young people leave East European countries looking for freedoms, we would do well to warn them that the gods of the West also have clay feet.

As I listened to exuberant comments of those crossing into the West, I couldn't help but wonder if their quest is fuelled by the desire to replace one form of materialism with another. Understandably, escape from the harassment of the KGB or the threat of the gulag is legitimate. But what is sought? The blessings of freedom in the West arise from political, social and economic structures which found their origin in a Christian understanding of life.

While eastern Europe seeks to rid itself of the demons of atheistic materialism, it needs to be warned that the demons of western materialism may be just as deceiving.

**The gods of the West
also have clay feet.**

24
Who Are the Good Guys?

It's difficult to admit we each see life through different windows

OKA USED TO be a pleasant, quiet place to visit. Occasionally Lily and I would leave our ministry tasks behind and take the ferry from the island of Montreal across to Oka for a drive in the countryside, more often than not stopping to buy cheese at the monastery just outside of town.

But quiet leisure is not what comes to mind when Oka is mentioned these days.

Fuelled by decades of frustration, accusations of dishonesty, a clash of cultures, and a new generation of impatient young natives, Oka entered the '90s as a bomb waiting for a light. Its fuse started burning in the summer of 1990.

The Oka conflict: who's right and who's wrong? It's easier to assess complex problems when there's a sharp contrast of black and white. Gray confuses the issue. Like a western movie, the plot is easier to follow if you know which cowboys are the good guys and which are the bad.

But how does one make sense of the conflict at Oka? Is it possible to distinguish the good guys from the bad guys?

Looking through windows

The window through which each of us views native Canada – and specifically the Oka confrontation – is shaped and coloured by our individual experience. Each of us has a bias which conditions our reaction.

Some of our windows are framed by the belief that natives have been totally misrepresented by the government. Romanticising the aboriginal plight, this view attributes native problems completely to governmental ignorance, incompetence and deliberate manipulation. Natives are viewed as victims, not at all responsible for their unfortunate situation. Those who disagree with this view are labelled "red necks."

Other Canadians, looking through a different type of window, perceive natives as lazy, living off of government hand-outs. Natives are characterized by their presence in the city streets, drunk and unkempt. Their disproportionately high incidence of crime only reinforces this stereotype. Through this window, natives are delinquent and debauched, completely responsible for their plight. Those who disagree with this perspective are labelled "bleeding hearts."

The blockades

The violence of the summer blockades, especially that of Oka, tends to sharpen the frames around the windows, entrenching the camps of both the "red necks" and the "bleeding hearts."

The seeming reluctance of both provincial and federal

governments to talk to native leaders reinforces the argument of governmental incompetence.

But at the same time, the criminal methods used by the Warriors reinforce the image of the unreasonable Indian, holding his automatic weapon, defending his right to run gambling casinos while calling for more government aid.

Beware of shutters

While each individual sees life through various windows of experience, personal disposition, political opinion and association, the Christian must also ask what a given situation looks like when framed by biblical values.

To close the shutters and ignore that we are living in a broken and fallen world is not only to err, but to sin. Each of us and each of our societies battles with the presence and activity of evil. We err when we decline responsibility for social breakdown and when we avoid involvement in human tragedy because "after all, it's someone else's problem." Or is secular society right when it declares that the gospel has no concern for the awful tragedy of the Canadian aboriginal?

Regardless of your point of view on Oka, concede with me that there exists a desperate situation. Without assigning fault, look out through a window that encompasses the whole nation and observe the sad conditions of a people who live in our midst.

The tragic facts

* Native young people between the ages of 15 and 24 are five to six times more likely to commit suicide.

* Twenty percent of all foster children in Canada are native, while natives compose only two percent of the child population.

* Thirty-five percent of full-blooded natives are in the lowest category of income: from nothing to $5,000 annually.

* Among non-native Canadians, eight percent die from violence, including fire, poison, drowning and other accidents. Among natives, 33 percent die from the same causes.

* In Manitoba, 35 percent of sexual abuse referrals involve status Indians, though they compose only six percent of the population.

We face an explosive situation. It is useless and naive to pretend that this situation will simply go away. Justifying one side or bias at the expense of the other is anything but helpful. If we want to sit around pointing fingers, I'm sure there is enough blame to go around. But right now action is needed. Action based on a reasoned understanding of the history and current tensions underlying the surface violence and anger.

Points to consider

Consider the incredible dislocation the European invasion imposed and continues to impose on aboriginals, shuttled off to small pockets of land in a country they used to roam freely.

Recognizing the hard lot of the natives, the Canadian government has attempted to compensate and appease this people. But governmental assistance to natives has served to create dependency, not encourage self-sufficiency. We must find ways of enhancing native financial autonomy. A number of native communities have already shown ability in creating and sustaining their own economies.

Our hungry development of natural resources, especially in industries such as mining, construction and energy, has not only further dislocated native groups, but has defeated itself economically by destroying the precious balance of nature which characterized these natural resources in the first place.

Those who have encountered governmental bureaucracy know the frustration of trying to elicit a decision from a civil servant. Multiply this frustration by many governments, both federal and provincial, over a few hundred years, and you begin to understand the aboriginal's fury; you begin to feel a build-up of frustration, packing down into anger and hostility.

Canada must wake up to the fact that colonization has failed. We are now facing the de-colonization of our aboriginal peoples. Many native people have taken up arms to declare their independence and to challenge any who oppose them.

And yet, despite the many injustices suffered by native Canada throughout history, it is dangerous to romanticize the aboriginal community, to see natives as perpetual victims and to rid them of any responsibility for consequences of their own choices. Gun-toting warriors, attempting to settle their grievances by armed force, cannot justly complain when their guns are met by other guns. To see natives as categorically blameless is to deny the spiritual fallenness in their own people and culture. They are sinners, just like the rest of us.

Finding a biblical window

My concern is that Christians don't simply mouth the opinions of the world without respect for the Word of God and its call for justice and mercy.

With the fallout at Oka, we are in danger of oversimplifying the issue: reacting to the criminal elements without recognizing the desperate call for help.

In my father's office hung a plaque with the words, "Great Spirit, grant that I may not criticize my neighbour until I have walked two miles in his moccasins."

Before you tell others how you see Oka through your window, ask a native person to describe what he or she sees.

**We must recognize
the desperate call for help.**

25
Abortion: Crisis of Leadership

Ultimately, the issue of the unborn is spiritual

I HEARD A MINISTER comment on a meeting to inform Christians on the struggle against abortion: "I don't want to subject my people to more blood and gore. Besides, my people have already made up their minds."

I confess that not long ago I shared those sentiments. I was trapped by assumptions that prevented my involvement. Today I see the issue differently. We are at a most critical moment, for the issue of the unborn is more than a legal or political concern; it is ultimately spiritual.

What are the assumptions that keep us from getting involved?

Excuses
1. It's a Roman Catholic issue. Since they are the ones who led the public debate and founded most pro-life organizations, many of us assumed there was nothing we could or should do.

2. If we speak truth, we have fulfilled our responsibility. Working from a theology that "God has spoken" leads us to assume that just speaking truth is sufficient.

3. God's will is being done. There's nothing we can really do.

4. My role is to protest against evil, not to legislate good.

5. There is nothing we can really do in this world because it is ruled by evil.

6. Our job is to save people from eternal punishment, not to correct today's public evil.

7. We already have a full agenda at our church. We don't have time to do more.

8. Let the pro-life organizations do the work.

9. I wrote a letter. What more do you want me to do?

A remarkable shift

Today, however, the issue has shifted. We see more clearly the consequences of the debate. As a result, church leaders must do more than just "take a stand" – they must exercise their spiritual leadership. Let me explain.

Historically the concern over abortion has been to protect the life of the unborn. Of course, this still is the primary concern. The advance of scientific technology, however, has enlarged that concern: tissue and organs from the unborn are now being used to heal the born. The fetal brain cell treatment of an adult Parkinson's disease patient, performed by British and American doctors, tells that story. By implanting cells from the brain of an aborted fetus into a man, doctors achieved a partial cure.

Spare parts

Such procedures are not only successful in curing disease but are also highly cost-effective. What this means is that the unborn are becoming a department of "spare parts."

Thus the debate has changed. No longer are we only trying to stop the death of the unborn. The future scenario is not only grotesque but also frightening. For if fetuses are regarded as non-human beings and therefore not entitled to protection, the unborn will be seen and used as a means of generating cells to renew the diseased parts of the born. And where will this practice lead us? A little imagination can paint the picture.

Today we are charged with the responsibility of arresting an immoral view of life itself. Given the possibility that fetal brain cells can also retard and cure Alzheimer's disease, the pressure from society to make fetal parts available will be enormous. We are standing at the top of a very slippery slope. Once society begins sliding down that slope it will be almost impossible to stop it.

In *Fragmented Gods*, sociologist Reginald Bibby claims that more than 20 percent of evangelicals (he uses the term conservative Protestants) favour abortion on demand.

Many evangelicals either have no understanding of this issue's serious implications or have opted for current secular thought. This calls us to inform our own people on the ultimate spiritual implications of this kind of thinking.

Pastors are overloaded

I appreciate the real problems of most church leaders. They are overloaded with responsibility. There is also a prevalent assumption that since the House of Commons has passed a bill there is nothing more that can be done. Although mistaken, this assumption leads the public to feel that the battle has been lost and further actions will be futile.

Misunderstanding combined with the general overload

of most local churches' agendas, simply snuffs out any energy or time which might be made available for involvement.

Needed: Leadership

Where do we turn today for leadership? The Roman Catholic Church has so many of its own institutions that it speaks mostly to its own people.

A real tragedy is that many of our mainline Protestant churches have opted to support the individual's personal choice on abortion, while others say little or nothing.

It's tragic but true that some leaders in pro-life movements by their strident and harsh approach have turned away many evangelicals from engagement.

We urgently need ministers who will:

a. Alert their people to the reality of the current crisis;

b. Free up some of their laity to act in the political arena;

c. Set aside funds to establish alternatives to abortion;

d. Work in fellowship with others, both locally and nationally, to set the course for future generations.

Let the battle not be lost because we did nothing. It is winnable. Perhaps not this year or next. But discouragement is not a fruit of the Spirit!

The unborn could become a department of "spare parts."

26
Supporting Imperfect Legislation

Is it biblical to support public policy that points in the right direction?

WHAT DO YOU do when a government proposes a bill that is going in the right direction but falls short of what you really want to support? This very situation arose in 1990 when the House of Commons debated bill C-43, a bill attempting to restrict the use of abortion in Canada.

The Evangelical Fellowship of Canada has consistently expressed its conviction regarding the need for protection of the unborn. Our extensive work in attempting to influence law makers and public opinion led us to respond to this bill directly. EFC's "Declaration on Human Life" calls for full protection of life, from conception to birth. We continue to press for that protection. In retrospect, I want to put the debate and bill into perspective.

Background
When the Supreme Court struck down Section 251 of the Criminal Code in 1988, it left no law to govern the use of

abortion in Canada. This led to a continuous and heated public protest, analysis by legal experts, commentary by spokespeople in the medical, religious, social and legal communities, heart-searching by politicians, sit-ins, jail sentences and voices of anger from all sides.

Finally the stage was set as the Members of Parliament filed in to record their final vote on Bill C-43. Before the vote was held a parliamentary committee heard numerous submissions from groups arguing for or against the bill or seeking to advance amendments to it.

The Members of Parliament were asked to pass or defeat the bill itself, apart from any changes before it would go to the Senate for further debate and, after that, for Royal Assent.

Along with my colleagues across Canada, I searched my heart, the Scriptures, legal arguments and opinions of respected associates and friends for a clear strategy with regard to abortion legislation. EFC produced a video, "Justice for All," arguing for the protection of the unborn from conception onward. I pressed for amendments, arguing that the bill, as it stood, was not strong enough. We also published a *National Alert* outlining arguments for and against.

Watching from the galleries

As I sat looking down from the galleries on the day of the final vote, I watched as the Members chatted with one another. Then the Speaker of the House rose to begin the vote. The house guards were very much in evidence; they carefully checked everyone upon entrance to the gallery for metal objects and then closely watched each person during the proceedings.

The Speaker called for MPs voting "yes" to stand. He

began with the Deputy Prime Minister, as the Prime Minister was away meeting with Mr. Gorbachev.

Then the vote call came to Kim Campbell, Minister of Justice. As she rose to indicate her "yes" vote, the galleries erupted with cries of protest. I was surprised at the anger of the protest and watched as the guards quickly removed the protesters. What struck me was the deep anger of those pro-choice voices as they protested against any bill that would restrict women's access to abortion. They screamed in rage and hurled insults as they were physically removed. Similar incidents occurred at least four times during the voting.

This experience was enlightening for me. The actions of the pro-choice demonstrators were not only a violation of the rules of the House but a sharp repudiation of the very laws of democracy which rule our society. (Democracy is not sacred. But it is the best form of political decision-making we know which respects the rights of citizens and at the same time provides a framework in which political decisions can be made.) As I sat in the House on that day I saw those, namely certain pro-choice advocates, who support the democratic system when expedient to their agenda choose anarchy when democracy is not very cooperative.

Astounded by the verbal violence as they shouted, it occurred to me that there may be good in this bill after all. If those who call for abortion on demand are against bill C-43, could it be that the bill indeed has merit?

What will the bill do?

We do not know how much the bill will restrict abortions. But we expect that hospitals and doctors will be reluctant to perform abortions for fear of legal action.

Watching as the vote was recorded, I was very conscious that this group of democratically elected persons in a secular and pluralistic society, operating within a democracy, were fumbling in an attempt to find a law that respects life. Bill C-43 is indeed a fumbling attempt, but an attempt nonetheless.

Even though this bill fails to bring about the protection we long and pray for, it is not appropriate to suggest that God is absent from the process.

This is not to say this bill is God's bill. Hardly! But we need to be reminded that the prayers of God's people are not ineffective. Daniel reminds us of this.

"He changes times and seasons; he sets up kings and deposes them. He gives wisdom to the wise, and knowledge to the discerning." (Daniel 2:21)

Why the anger?

So why are pro-choicers so angry with the bill? In my view it's because the bill has changed the very assumptions underlying the debate. When Jake Epp, a senior member of the cabinet, argued with the Prime Minister that the gestation approach was wrong, Epp's persuasive defense of the unborn pulled the rug out from under the pro-choice arguments.

The gestation approach, embraced by many within the pro-choice community, dictates that abortion is acceptable during the early stages of pregnancy (in Canada up to 24 weeks). Abortions performed later in the pregnancy than the allotted period are deemed to be unacceptable. Based on the gestation approach, legislative bodies need only concern themselves with establishing "reasonable" time constraints.

Different ground rules

The ground rules are different now: the issue is no longer one of time but of circumstance. Bill C-43 works from the assumption that the unborn cannot be aborted unless certain conditions are met. It is here that the bill is very weak and in my view fumbles; I don't believe the conditions governing abortion are stringent enough. It will take a tremendous amount of political and legal effort to strengthen the bill.

But the inadequacy of Bill C-43 should not blind us to the fact that the ground rules underlying the abortion debate have changed. And it's my opinion that, quite apart from Bill C-43, these new ground rules better serve as a basis for pro-life legislation. That's why those supporting unlegislated abortion are angry. They've lost the foundational assumptions that gave them abortion without restriction.

The best we can get?

I do, however, have difficulties with the argument used by some pro-lifers, that "this bill is the best we can get so let's get it while we can."

In a broken and fallen world, God's will is that His "shalom" (a Hebrew word encompassing His righteousness and justice) rules. Thus, our choices must be made in alignment with His will.

The point of political action for the Christian is not getting what I can today; rather, it's helping to bring about God's "shalom." If a piece of legislation moves in the direction of His "shalom," then it's right; if not, then it's wrong. The question here is not one of degree or distance but of direction.

The abortion issue will not go away with the passing of

any bill. The passage of any bill respecting abortion will serve to refuel the debate.

The battle is not over

My prayer is that Christians will become even more active in ministries that combat the circumstances giving rise to abortions. These would include crisis pregnancy centres, homes for un-wed mothers, low cost housing and counselling.

The writer of the Hebrews said of Christ, "You have loved righteousness and hated wickedness; therefore God, your God, has set you above your companions."

While we identify evil, let us also be known as those who encourage goodness. There are times when reaction must give way to pro-action.

**In darkness,
whenever you see
a flickering candle,
fan the flame.**

27
Lessons from an Abortionist and an AIDS Victim

Can we really change our world without sacrifice?

IT WAS JUST a simple dinner in a quiet downtown hotel room. Nothing unusual, except the guest was a man many Canadians either love or despise – Dr. Henry Morgentaler. The dinner been had arranged in a private room so no one would know we were there. Especially the press. We wanted to converse in quiet surroundings without the usual posturing, name calling and shouts of hostility, so typical of some media encounters with Dr. Morgentaler.

We had arranged the meeting for several reasons: To witness of the Lord Jesus and express love to Dr. Morgentaler and then to explain why we believe justice for the unborn is so critical.

Dr. Morgentaler talked about his early years when his parents had turned from Judaism to communism. He recalled when his father was killed by the Nazis in Poland. He described the capture and death of his mother and sister in Auschwitz and then the four years he and his brother lived in both Auschwitz and Dachau. It was there he embraced humanism as his system of belief.

Our time began with a prayer before dinner and a personal prayer for Henry. Our conversation at times became heated and animated. At the end I saw no indication that his mind was changed in any way. It was clear that he sees himself as a crusader for the rights of women.

Learning some lessons

My commitment to biblical justice for the unborn, however, was strengthened. Although I stand in opposition to his view of life, I was deeply challenged by his willingness to risk jail for his convictions. To many Canadians he has become a hero because of his determination to risk his own freedom. Some may say he does it for the money. But that, to me, is cynicism. The lesson for evangelicals is that too often we assume we can change our world without a sacrifice. Jesus calls us to risk everything for His kingdom.

There was another lesson for me. The CBC's The Journal, hosted by Barbara Frum, invited me to be on a panel of scientific, medical and legal experts to discuss AIDS. Included on the panel was Allan, a homosexual with AIDS.

When Barbara introduced me and used the word "evangelical," the audience of some 300 booed. This only affirmed to me the reason I was there: to state publicly evangelicals' concern about the consequence of violating moral laws.

After a brief preamble, I asked the question, "Because we know that 74 percent of the transmission of the AIDS virus is within a particular community (medical experts confirm that three-fourths of transmission is by homosexual intercourse), isn't it time we face the music and admit that the most obvious way to stop the spread of AIDS is to cease the homosexual lifestyle?"

While I spoke, I noticed that Allan turned to me with a look that seemed to say, "Oh sure, you self-righteous evangelical!" I was troubled. Was he offended because he knew I opposed his moral views, or had he only heard evangelicals shout at him?

After the taping I walked to the front and worked my way over to where Allan was standing. He seemed surprised to see me. I put my arm around him, and in simple faith, prayed, asking for his healing, and then I stepped back.

"But, Brian," he said. "I'm a Buddhist."

"Allan, you're God's creation and he cares for you," I said. "I'll continue to pray for God's intervention in your life."

He smiled. A watery film covered his eyes. I walked away.

The disease of AIDS connected to the issue of homosexuality is very disconcerting. But at that moment God reminded me that Jesus gave his life for people in need.

It's one thing to proclaim the truth of God and righteousness from the mountaintop. However, there comes a time when I must walk the valleys of human need, suffering and sin.

What Jesus did

Jesus, reaching back into the book of Isaiah, said, "The Spirit of the Lord is upon me. Because He anointed me to preach the gospel to the poor. He has sent me to proclaim release to the captives and recovery of sight to the blind. To set free those who are downtrodden. To proclaim the favourable year of the Lord."

In an age of encroaching secularism, the rise of humanism and the deterioration of moral attitudes, we can too easily be trapped by our own feelings. It's one thing to know the cause. It's something else to walk in a world of diseased lives. It's those who are ill who need a physician.

These two encounters have strengthened my resolve to be an active part of God's kingdom and bring His truth to this age. But may I never forget that along with the call to "proclaim release," to bring "recovery of sight" and "set free," comes a responsibility to walk beside the "poor," the "captives," the "blind" and the "downtrodden." In short, to give my life to those in need.

**We must not only
proclaim God's truth
but walk the valleys
of human need.**

28
The Erosion of Influence

Losing prayer in the public schools symbolizes a larger loss

AT SUPPER ONE evening our daughter recounted some disturbing events of that day at high school: school prayers and Bible reading had been eliminated from the schedule.

The Ontario Court of Appeal had struck down a regulation requiring school boards to hold prayers during their opening exercises. It had ruled that the Education Act's section on prayer was an infringement of the rights to freedom of conscience and religion.

To many of us, this decision did not come as a shock. It's further confirmation of the erosion of Christian influence in our public schools over the past few years. But how could I explain to my daughter the logic of those who made the decision?

It's not easy. What might be obvious to me as a parent who has watched the increased secularism of our culture doesn't make much sense to a young person used to certain patterns and affirmations.

The real story
What is the real story behind the disallowance of prayer in public schools? The court has made it clear. In its view, our society is no longer founded on Judeo-Christian faith, and therefore it will not allow the prayers of the majority to be conducted in a publicly funded institution.

Some claim the reason for the edict is the assimilation of various non-Christian religions into our culture over the past few decades. While our country has certainly become more multicultural, giving higher visibility to other faiths, it is unfair to use this as the reason biblical morality is no longer fundamental to our society. In my view, that's a smoke screen.

The force that has blunted the role of Christian faith in society is secularism – the idea that God is irrelevant to life, including education.

Secularism
Even though a high percentage of Canadians believe in a personal God and in Jesus as the Son of God, we have divided life into two segments, "secular" and "sacred." This dichotomy allows our culture, including the educational system, to build its assumptions of truth apart from Christian ideas. Religion is seen as a curious part of our culture; interesting but not essential.

How did secularism become dominant? One reason, which we as evangelicals are quite unwilling to admit, is that for much of this century, many of us have been absent from affirming Christian truth and values in the marketplace.

Because of that absence, when it came time for Christian faith to help weave the fabric of the educational curriculum, we simply were not there.

Pluralism

As "secularism" is the idea that predominantly shapes our decision-making, "pluralism" is the way we make decisions.

Picture a number of people sitting at a round table with each person representing a different view. The discussion that ensues makes two assumptions: first, that because there are a variety of opinions (a plurality of views), no one view is therefore correct; and second, that religious views are not tolerated (it's here that secularism takes over). The latter assumption is hardly ever stated but is there, nevertheless.

Dr. Paul Marshall, author of *Thine is the Kingdom* (IVP), puts it this way: A high school principal looks around his school and says, "Some like to play hockey, others prefer football and still others would rather have soccer. Given the various preferences, I will not allow any sports."

The rationale in our pluralistic society is that because there are differences, no one group – especially the majority – is allowed special status, such as having Christian prayer in public institutions.

On the other side of the issue, we might ask whether prayers in the schools have really served us well in transmitting the truth of the gospel to young people. Or have we been duped into thinking that our public schools have been "Christian"? If the value of school prayers has been minimal, what have we really lost?

The real loss

To me, the real loss has been Christian leadership, not only in the schools but in the country at large. The loss of school prayer is symbolic of the larger loss.

What can we do to ensure that Christ's message is heard

by our students? We can become so preoccupied with our supposed "right" to have prayer in the schools that the primary issue of communicating Christ gets lost in the shuffle.

We assumed we had immediate access into our schools. And so while we spend millions of dollars on communicating Christ to people of other languages and cultures, we drive by our schools forgetting they are filled with young people lost without Christ.

How do we as the followers of Christ respond, not only to the disallowance of prayer in the schools, but to the bigger issue of God's being excluded from life?

We march to the beat of a different drummer. Our orders come from our Father. That isn't intolerance; it's religious integrity.

But how do we march to the beat of a different drummer? Some feel justified by reacting in anger and outright hostility. Others pack their bags and slip away into the night deciding to ignore the culture. Both responses are unacceptable.

We acknowledge that pluralism is the operative word in Canada. It simply means that the monolithic view of biblical morality is being replaced with a pluralistic view which holds that no single religious doctrine can be used for writing a Canadian law or establishing social conventions.

That is what the Supreme Court has affirmed in various decisions. Tragically, we have lost the fundamental base that has brought such blessing and benefit to this country.

However, we are called by Christ to be faithful to Him in a changing world. Like Christ's followers in other countries, we must learn to serve and uphold His name in the face of hostilities, be it pluralism or secularism.

How did I answer my daughter at the dinner table that night? By reminding her that, prayers or no prayers, in her school she must shine as Christ's light – but now even more brightly.

**Christians march
to the beat
of a different drummer.**

29
The Feminist Critique: Hype or Reality?

The Montreal massacre – how do we fathom this despicable act?

CANADA FORMALLY ANNOUNCED its loss of innocence when Marc Lepine carried a semi-automatic gun into the University of Montreal and, coolly separating the women from the men, shot and killed 14 female students in December of 1989. In the past, Canadians have assumed that this kind of violence happened only south of the border. We now know differently.

The main debate rising out of this massacre is not about the need for gun control laws, as one might expect. It's about the role of feminism in society, and male reaction to feminist concerns, criticisms and goals.

The pro-feminist and at times anti-male rhetoric which poured forth following the Montreal murders has generated, on one side, sympathy and understanding, and on the other, a sense that feminist response has blown the gender conflict in Canada out of proportion.

Michelle Landsberg wrote in the *Toronto Star*:

"In your town and mine, in every town in this country, violent woman-hating is a daily truth. 'Marc' was insane. But his murderous rage took the path it so often takes in our society: it targeted women. Women are generally smaller, unlikely to strike back, and they're available. Right now in Canada women's bones are being cracked, their eyes blackened, arms twisted, minds and hearts stabbed with abusive words. When a man in a rage goes hunting for a victim, nine times out of ten he hunts for a woman . . . any woman."

Across the country, in cities and towns, thousands of women, along with men, stood in silent vigils grieving the terrible loss of 14 lives. Many of the speeches echoed the now familiar phrase, "feminism is the great unkept promise of democracy."

I have been thrown back and forth on these wild waves of debate. My first reaction was grief. I have for years been disturbed by the seeming non-response of evangelical leaders to the increased plight of women and girls who are brutalized and traumatized by men. We have been unwilling to stand up in defence of women or to develop and implement strategies to assist the female victims in our homes, neighbourhoods and even our churches.

Are all men guilty?
But I'm also annoyed by those who insist on linking all men to Marc Lepine: those who implicate all men in this bloody massacre because Lepine, as his note says, blamed feminist advocates for his failures.

On CBC's Morningside, host Peter Gzowski protested a woman's claim that all men are chauvinists. He asserted that, while this was indeed a horrible tragedy for women, it was also a tragedyfor men.

Writer Thomas Walkom took the debate in another direction. He blamed this killing on the current social context of what he calls "neo-conservatism." He wrote in the *Toronto Star*:

"Neo-conservatism began as anti-communism and has gravitated to anti-liberalism. Increasingly, it has focused on what its proponents call morality and family values. In religion, it is fundamentalism. Its great crusade has become the fight against abortion.

"The Canadian version is also suspicious of Quebec, anti-immigrant and warm to the U.S. But increasingly, its centre pin has become anti-feminism."

For Walkom, Lepine represents neo-conservative ideals. We must avoid the trap Walkom has fallen into. Reacting to a reaction is neither helpful nor Christ-like. But the question calling for a response is, What are we to understand from the unspeakable shame of this despicable act?

Lessons

The first lesson is to avoid reacting to shrill feminist hype. If we condone strident anti-feminism, we neglect a significant number of Canadian woman and men who are grieved by a lack of equity in society. It would be simple and convenient to label these equity-minded Canadians as liberal, leftist, socialistic secularists, who attempt to thwart godliness and biblical faith. But the fact is, many women within our churches are asking that men sit up and rethink male and female roles in the church and the home.

My plea to pastors and male church leaders is that we do not simplistically reject these feminist concerns. Underneath every extreme social movement – strident and obnoxious though it may seem – lies a cankerous need.

A naive and simplistic analysis of social problems

would want us to regard these problems as cleanly two-sided: feminism against traditional family values, conservatism against liberalism, secularism against religious faith, women against men, and women's rights activists against the traditional biblical role of women. In this over-simplified world view, each camp assumes that it is right, the other is wrong and that there is no middle ground.

His example

As followers of Christ we cannot afford to be trapped into assuming that the two sides in any given debate are mutually exclusive. Such a division does not represent Christ.

Jesus refused to be owned by any neatly packaged side. His moral distance as prophet allowed Him to pronounce judgment on issues of his age without any hint of collusion. His love for the individual allowed Him to comfort and heal regardless of the person's belief or behaviour.

As His followers, we are to oppose evil wherever we find it, be it an anti-female joke in the mouth of a church leader or a racist joke told by a colleague. Both depreciate God's creation and are therefore evil.

Lepine reminded us of the violence and sexism of this age: a world in which Rambo movies gross millions; children idolize brutish wrestlers; popular broadcasters promote sock'em, punch'em hockey; beer commercials laud the pick-up strategy of men in a bar; and numerous newspapers across Canada insist on a daily pin-up girl.

While the horror of the Montreal massacre cannot be reduced to a purely male/female issue, it does remind us of the widespread abuse of women in this generation. I reject the attempt to link these killings with anyone who does not buy into the full agenda of the feminist movement. But at the same time I'm mindful of the fear and anger written on the faces of those who attended vigils, and I acknowledge that sexism is partly to blame for the fuelling of this fear and anger – sexism that is woven into our societal values and norms.

In its attempt to deal with unfair accusations against men and conservatism, the evangelical church has not been particularly sensitive to the pain or social implications of this tragedy. Do we need to be reminded that Jesus was light years ahead of the male chauvinism of His day as He gave dignity to women as equal members of His world? May the evangelical church in this age do no less than Christ. May we give full place to women, that which is God's by creation – His very image.

**The church has generally failed
to assist female victims
in our homes, neighbourhoods
and churches.**

30
Pornography's Monstrous Lie

Do anti-pornography laws violate the right to free speech?

THERE IS AN ironic twist to today's human rights movement. It's being used to support the marketing of the lie that anti-pornography laws violate the right to free speech. Indeed, "human rights" has become a cloak for those who oppose any form of censorship and it's used by the industry to support its unhindered rights to make money any way it chooses.

Censorship has become a nasty word, especially in places such as South Africa, Nicaragua and the Soviet Union. It sounds very progressive to allow publishers to print what they want without governmental interference.

Victims
But what about the victims of the lies? Implicit in the magazines and films of the pornographic industry are some heinous assumptions: Women are for the pleasure of men; women enjoy rape and bondage; men are animalistic,

driven by a raging, physical lust; children are matured by experiencing sexual play with adults; sexual pleasure in marriage can be enhanced by other sex partners; and life is better when people give vent to pornographic fantasies.

Surely we saw the variegated leaf of human rights in a trial in which a publisher was convicted of printing lies about Jews and distorting the history of the holocaust. Some asserted that the free speech rights of the publisher were violated. But it was not his rights that were at stake; rather, the rights of the people he wrote about.

This, to me, is also what's at stake in the pornography debate. Are we willing to allow the pornography industry to continue as a lie machine, fabricating distortions about human life and spewing out its sewage, all wrapped in the garb of human rights?

Columnist Michele Landsberg said it this way:

"The civil libertarians and pornographers will have the most free speech in the debate, and the victims of pornography will have the least. As always, the free-speechers will try to silence the anti-pornographers by *ad feminism* insult ('housewife,' 'prude,' 'anti-sex,' and 'fundamentalist' will be the most common and shaming terms of personal abuse) and the media, which naturally have an enormous financial and ideological stake in unfettered liberty, will give far more free speech to the free-speechers than to their opponents."

A senior policy advisor for a government minister said that after seeing a series of clips the RCMP had taken from porno flicks available on the open market, it took months to erase from his memory the distortions he had seen. If this is true for a seasoned Christian and family man, imagine the effect on someone who knows nothing about the battle of evil and good and the work of Christ to forgive and transform.

A reporter asked me if we were trying to return our society to a prudish, anti-sex era. My response was, "it's not our intent to go back to some nostalgic 'good old days.' But neither will we sit by and allow society to legalize lies about life. We want to warn our culture that there are consequences."

Listen to the stories

I'd like those who advocate a pornographic open market to come with me to a home for battered wives and hear the stories of women whose souls and bodies have been devastated by men crazed with desire for sordid experiments.

I'd like them to hear the stories of two men who shared their burdens with me, burdens born out of fascination with pornography. One is struggling to get his wife and child to return home. Why did she leave? Because of the neurotic sexual behaviour of her husband who wanted to mimic what he had seen. The second is unmarried, driven almost to suicide by the compulsive habit of years of filling his mind with lust.

Why is it that for many little girls, it's more dangerous to be in their beds at home than wandering the streets? It's because heterosexual men are driven to work out their "needs" and fantasies on those too weak to protect themselves. And why are men so out of control? One very good reason is that the lies of pornography perpetuate a myth, which many men have completely embraced.

I wouldn't dare even print the names of some pornographic magazines. Loaded with four-letter-type insinuations, they are part of the dark side of our North American culture – another example of the battle of the demonic.

Yet in the face of this unspeakable shame, hypocrisy at

the highest level is made fashionable. Who mounts the high horse of respectability, demanding the rights offered by our democratic society? Is it the victims of the lie? No. Rather, it's those who mistakenly think the quality of life is advanced by unbounded expression and by those who stand to gain from pumping forth the magazines and videos.

This is a moment when silence is not golden.

There is an edge to the cliff.
When you go too far,
there are consequences.

31
To Save Seals or Souls?

Why are evangelicals reluctant to support environmental concerns?

TIME DEDICATED ITS 1989 magazine of the year to "planet earth." The cover depicted the globe, wrapped in plastic, under environmental siege.

We're finally waking up to a horrible reality: that when we violate God's principles by ravaging the earth, all humans pay the consequences.

For too long evangelicals have ignored issues on the environment. I believe this has occurred for two primary reasons.

First, environmental groups such as Greenpeace often seem to be coming from the "left." As a result we're reluctant to support the same issues they do, even if we agree with their analyses. Were we to agree publicly with them we could be accused of siding with their humanistic approach.

For example, if we support the protection of whales, or picket against acid rain or complain about the polluting of our waters, some immediately assume we're also anti-business and pro-abortion. In short, protecting our environment is seen as being on the side of the "humanists." Lost, of course, is the biblical reality, "The earth is the Lord's and the fullness thereof."

The second reason has to do with our eschatology. Given our expectation of Christ's soon return and the eventual restructuring of "the new heaven and the new earth," we believe there is no need to "waste our time" on the environment; better, instead, to prepare people for life after death.

These problems are very real for me. I find the attitudes and behaviour of Greenpeace and other groups to be often antagonistic. While they protest the killing of whales and baby seals, they have not, to my knowledge, cried out against the killing of unborn humans. Further, they seem to suggest that business itself is inherently evil. For me, the thought of working with such groups is repugnant. Their reason for preserving the environment is humanistic; i.e., humankind is god.

Moreover, I believe in the imminent, literal return of Jesus Christ. He will utterly defeat evil and His kingdom will reign over all of life. Thus, to prepare people for eternity is of vital importance. To live on this planet is not the sum of life. We are preparing for eternity.

What to do?

So what do I do? Can I set the preservation of the planet as a high priority? How can I stand for things that others, with whom I have fundamental disagreement, also support? Is it a violation of Christ's call to "go into all the world and proclaim the gospel" when I protest against the destruction of rain forests, which in turn upsets the earth's atmosphere? What I have just pointed out is a false dichotomy. It's a problem but it's a false problem. It exists in my mind, not in the universe, of which Christ is Lord.

Follow the argument by considering this example. As parents, my wife and I accept our responsibility to provide for the physical needs of our children. We feed, clothe, house and school them. They are never malnourished nor do they freeze in the cold. But is that the end of our task? Surely we've provided for the essentials. But our children are not just physical beings. What about their emotional health, the education of their minds and the development of their gifts? Aren't those also the parents' responsibility?

The danger here is called reductionism. While being a parent involves providing food, clothing and shelter, our task can't be reduced to that alone. There is much more involved.

So it is with being Christ's followers on this planet in this age. Our mandate is as broad as His concerns. To reduce our role to a single statement of Christ is to be trapped by reductionism.

Extremes

But being human, we shift from one extreme to another. For example, earlier this century, proponents of the "social gospel" got trapped into reducing the issue of sin. Believing that the real problem of society lay in evil societal structures, they tended to discount the matters of personal evil and wickedness.

"To bring the Kingdom of God to society you must therefore change the structures," they said. That's how the modern NDP party got its start, at least in the prairies.

And what did evangelicals do? We reduced the problem of sin on the other side. We said, "The real problem is that individuals are in need of personal salvation; it has nothing to do with the structures of society." We ended up preaching a personal salvation with little or no attempt to change those elements of society that destroy both the spirit and body.

Living at the end of this century, we are faced with the devastating fact that our planet is on its last legs. Regardless of the "when and how" of your eschatology, we're still left with the reality that this planet is part of God's creation. And Christ's command "to make disciples" does not countermand his command to "Be fruitful and multiply, and fill the earth, and subdue it; and rule over the fish of the sea and over the birds of the sky, and over every living thing that moves on the earth."

These two commands of our God exist side by side. Our task is not complete when we have won everyone to Christ. That's one side. Nor are we to care only about the environment and ignore the eternal lostness of people without Christ.

The word "environment" is not owned by Greenpeace any more than the word "love" is owned by Hollywood. Environment speaks of God's world and love speaks of God's heart. Let's not allow others to take over an agenda that is rightfully ours as children of Planet Earth's Creator.

**Regardless of the "when and how"
of Christ's return,
this planet is still
part of God's creation.**

32
Humanitarianism
Is Not Enough

Are we prepared to add an adjective
to "humanitarianism"?

WHEN ROCK SINGER Bob Geldof organized Live Aid, a
worldwide rock concert to raise money for starving peoples, he helped to make the feeding of Ethiopians headline
news. His efforts even earned him a Nobel Peace prize
nomination. Since then Farm Aid and even Whisky Aid
have been on the bandwagon of humanitarianism.

Religious agencies specializing in humanitarian assistance benefited from this media hype as millions of dollars
poured in. Humanitarianism is becoming big business.

The Canadian International Development Agency
(CIDA) recognizes that money channelled through religious groups is often used more efficiently than monies
sent to governments. As the profile and credibility of
Christian humanitarian agencies increase, both government and the public will want Christian humanitarian
agencies to fill the role as world helpers.

But what are the expectations? How can evangelically

based organizations, whether international groups or local city missions, respond? Will there be expectations that Christian humanitarian groups, in a shift toward feeding the starving and healing the hurting, will in effect drop their evangelical world view? Could the pressure of being good, caring citizens compromise the ultimate spiritual objectives of an agency? Is humanitarianism seen as being kind to our world neighbours without affirming basic doctrines of sin, salvation and eternity? Is it enough to feed and clothe?

In effect, is humanitarianism enough?

Is it enough?

For evangelicals, humanitarianism alone is not enough. As important as they are, feeding the hungry, caring for the homeless, building hospitals, rebuilding economies and structuring social nets are not enough. Indeed, Jesus calls us to serve people, regardless of their beliefs or spiritual responses.

Even as we do these things, we're often seen not as being religious but as enlightened. But the gospel of Jesus Christ calls us to go beyond "enlightened humanity." Regardless of how informed our current culture may seem to be, a Christian world view calls us to position human need within a larger scene, to understand that life on this planet and within this framework of time is part of something bigger.

The danger is that we conform to societal expectations by delivering goods and services in the pursuit of meeting human need, but we either ignore or camouflage our opinion that mankind is lost and in need of a Saviour. Usually it's not that there is a denial of faith, but the faith aspect can be mere tokenism; we support our literature or media campaigns with religious language, but in essence we operate as just another agency, meeting the agenda of a world that wants the benefits of Christ's love without Christ's analysis or remedy.

James' succinct description of religion reads thus: "Religion that God our Father accepts as pure and faultless is this: to look after orphans and widows in their distress and to keep oneself from being polluted by the world" (James 1:27).

Making a response

He calls for two levels of response: the heart (feeling the needs of those around us) and the mind ("seeing" what is true). One can't work without the other. If only the heart is operating, one can too easily slip into emotional trivia. Yet intellectual awareness will leave one cold and analytical.

Evangelicals, at least during the earlier part of this century, too often have been guilty of only "seeing." Physical need was disregarded because heaven was the only appropriate solution to human need.

"Love in the biblical sense is compassion that embraces sinners in their misery, not toleration that respects others despite their sin," says theologian Donald G. Bloesch. "Love is less a rational esteem than a holy madness driving one to sacrifice one's own interest and welfare for the good of others. Love in the Christian sense is not prudent and calculating but ecstatic and overflowing, or as Bernard of Clairvaux puts it, 'impetuous, vehement, burning.' " [1]

In recent years there has been a renewed attitude within the evangelical community fostering a deeper commitment to Christian humanitarianism.

That, however, is the reason for my concern. Are we prepared to add an adjective to humanitarianism?

A warning

Bloesch warns that "when concern for social improvement pre-empts the hope for the righteousness of the kingdom, we are in the humanitarian rather than the biblical thought-world. The focus is no longer on the deliverance of humanity by a divine Saviour but on rebuilding humanity. While the humanist seeks only to improve the world, the evangelical seeks a new world, a new heaven and a new earth." [2]

This does not mean we cannot or should not work alongside people who could be called secular humanitarians. CIDA, local governments and agencies who have no "kingdom" interest but authentically care for people in need, are compatible with evangelicals on the short term. In fact, in many cases we can combine forces to achieve particular goals.

But as our immediate goals coincide with secular humanitarians we must be aware of the subtlety of being pressured to stay within their narrow definition of humanitarianism. The pressure can especially be felt when money is involved. It's tempting to gain the approval of the media, government and the public by upholding only those goals that are in accord with their secular humanitarianism, while downplaying the higher realities of the gospel.

Sometimes I'm shamed by the sterling dedication of those who make no pretence of Christian convictions. They'll go to unbelievable lengths to love and care for those in need, without any return, often putting to shame those who are called by the name of Christ. They genuinely want to bring hope and assistance to others.

Yet good works are not necessarily Christian and do not make one a Christian. A Christian is motivated to do good works out of thankfulness to a God of mercy and grace. Religious faith is not a function of ethics; rather, ethics should be an expression of faith.

Secular humanitarianism, regardless of its human benefit, is based on an ultimate trust in the goodness of man.

Seduced by applause

As Christian humanitarian agencies become more popular they will increasingly be faced with the challenge of how they'll educate the tens of thousands who look to them for direction. They face the danger of being seduced by the public's applause of good works or assuming that good works are good enough. As well, they can be baited by the false notions that improving people's condition is the same as establishing the kingdom of Christ or that current dilemmas have nothing to do with the bondage of evil or spiritual death.

Gandhi said, "In my judgment the Christian faith does not lend itself to much preaching or talking. It is best propagated by living it and applying it . . . When will you Christians really crown [Jesus Christ] as the Prince of Peace and proclaim him throughout your deeds as the champion of the poor and oppressed?" [3]

He is partially correct. The Christian message is demonstrated by the way we live. And Jesus did champion the cause of the poor and oppressed. But to say that was His primary mission is to completely miss the central purpose of his coming. Further, it equates Jesus as being just another good and effective moral leader. Such a conclusion is misleading.

It equally needs to be stated that evangelicals can be too easily trapped by unbiblical assumptions such as, "saving souls doesn't call for caring for the entire person," or "serving justice is less significant than winning a person to Jesus Christ." It's also wrong to assert that Christ does not care about nations, economies or the health of people, or that a nonbeliever is any less the object of God's care and love.

The world is watching. We do glorify God by our good works. To be a Christian humanitarian is to care for people because they, like we, have an eternal destiny and because Christ calls us to be His hand extended. There is no escaping His clear mandate.

"And what does the Lord require of you? To act justly and to love mercy and to walk humbly with your God" (Micah 6:8).

Humanitarianism is a good word and one worth saving. But in today's jungle of words, the snare of what others want us to be calls for us to keep our eyes wide open. Adding "Christian" as an adjective not only keeps us on the right trail but signals to others who we really are.

**Subtle pressures to compromise
can reduce our Christian witness
to mere tokenism.**

[1] *Faith and Its Counterfeits*, D. G. Bloesch, IVP, 1981, p.48
[2] Ibid., p.50
[3] *What Do You Say to a Hungry World?* S. Mooneyham, Word Books, p. 243, 1975.

33
Science Boxed In

Where the Rushton-Suzuki
"superior race" debate breaks down

THE TEMPERATURE ROSE as geneticist and television commentator Dr. David Suzuki angrily denounced psychologist and professor Dr. Philip Rushton. The crowd was clearly cheering for Suzuki. Outside the university hall angry students protested against Rushton's theories about intelligence while inside one scientist attempted to discredit another's views by sharp attack.

The scientists' much-publicized debate in London, Ontario in 1989 and the controversy surrounding it stemmed from a research paper by Rushton. In it he asserted that there are genetic differences among the major human races which cause variations in their average intelligence. Orientals, he argued, are more "highly evolved" – more advanced – than whites, and whites more so than blacks. These genetic differences, according to Rushton, have developed over hundreds of thousands of years of evolutionary history.

At the outset, let me make it clear that I disagree with Rushton's rationale (which is based on evolutionary theory) as well as with his conclusions. I find repugnant his assertion of racial superiority. But I was intrigued by the anger and indignation of those – especially the academic and scientific community – who oppose Rushton's theory.

When scientific theories clash

The Rushton-Suzuki debate focused, ironically, on the appearance that Rushton's conclusions seemed to be implicitly racist rather than on whether or not Rushton's actual research methods were valid.

Nevertheless, the clash between the two scientists serves to reveal the bankruptcy of scientific research which ignores or denies the sacred. A geneticist who believes in the equality of races runs headlong into the views of a psychologist who begins with Suzuki's assumptions about life's origin but ends with opposing conclusions.

Their debate got bogged down because neither scientist took the discussion back far enough – to examine the assumptions underlying their theories about life's origin.

Secular science's blind spot

We must begin at the beginning. Suzuki's and Rushton's shared assumption is that people (*homo sapiens*) emerged amid a cosmos whose beginning had no external impetus. The problem is that if creation is self-contained, the meaning of creation must also be found within itself. To define the nature and purpose of life with reference to a force or being outside the physical realm is to Suzuki and Rushton religious, thus unscientific and therefore untenable.

But when nothingness is the starting point, and random chance the process, who can say that one race evolving in the Orient may not be further advanced than another in Europe or Africa? If there is no ultimate source of human nature, why is it not feasible that one race might evolve more quickly than another and end up higher on the evolutionary scale?

Suzuki calls such an idea "bad science" – preposterous and unthinkable. But what are his grounds? Since both scientists begin with the same premise about life's origin, both must deny that there is something inherent in the human race which determines that people, apart from obvious physical differences, are essentially equal.

For Suzuki to suggest such would be to admit there is something special about the human species which guarantees that people are equal.

But to admit as much would be to upset the rationale of modern evolutionary thought. Such rationale postulates that present life forms on our planet came from the haphazard and random interchange of gases and chemicals.

Why racism is wrong

While I support Suzuki's disdain for racism, I do so for different reasons. I affirm the essential equality of human beings not because I am repulsed by racism – which I am – or because I believe I have a firmer grasp of genetics than Rushton. My reason is that I know human life is a direct expression of a living and self-revealing God. Racism is wrong because it distorts God's creation by refusing to recognize its source and purpose.

Suzuki is trapped by his argument: that comparing the average aptitudes and intelligences of races (if such a thing can be done) is wrong because of the possible conclusions that could be drawn from the findings. One could ask, Why is it not reasonable and indeed important in terms of the progress of ideas to examine races for possible reasons for their differences?

The dilemma in this current controversy is, of course, not new. Earlier this century, European philosopher Friedrich Nietzsche spun his webbed theory of the "superman," which he based on Darwin's theory of evolution. He proposed that the evolving of our species in a godless world resulted in beings that were qualitatively different, some superior to others. He chose the Aryan race as superior to all others. History tells the rest.

Hitler took Nietzsche's concept of a super race and built upon it a political empire which had as its central tenet, racial superiority. He also determined his own laws of morality in a world without God.

It was reported that Hitler instructed his soldiers to carry in their fieldsacks a copy of Nietzsche's writings and encouraged the practise of eugenics (the attempt to improve a race by selective breeding). Those considered genetically inferior – Jews, gypsies and homosexuals – were sent to the death camps. Soon after Hitler's rise to power, 225,000 "undesirables" were sterilized, 94,000 mental patients were killed and another 100,000 were left to die. Soldiers were encouraged to father children as often as they could, especially with biologically fit women.

When God is denied

All of this was done in the mad attempt to improve what Nazis thought was the superior race. And what was this philosophy's source? Not a scientific theory but a pagan view of life. When the transcendent is discounted, any theory is possible.

Theories have real impact. When unleashed, they ripple across a society, at times with ferocious impact. Yes,

Suzuki is justified in fearing the consequences of Rushton's theories: they are frightful.

But it does little good to flail at the air, pronouncing the evil of it all. What must be attacked are the fundamental assumptions which allow those ideas to rear their ugly heads.

Science is a major religion in our time. The Scientific Method has become our culture's Ten Commandments, the research laboratory our temple, the scientist our high priest and scientific discoveries our manna.

Commenting on the attempts of American scientists to create SDI (Strategic Defense Initiative) to shield the West from the East, someone said, "This is not technology but theology!"

And so are the theories of Rushton and Suzuki. They begin with no starting point but secular speculation. As G. K. Chesterton commented, "When you believe in nothing you can believe in anything. "

**When the transcendent
is discounted,
any theory is possible.**

idolatry